The Evolution

of

FIQH

(Islamic law & The Madh-habs)

By
Dr. Abu Ameenah Bilal Philips

ISLAMIC BOOK SERVICE

The Evolution of FIQH
(Islamic law & Madh-habs)
by Dr. Abu Ameenah Bilal Philips
e-mail: abuameenah@bilalphilips.com

ISBN: 81-7231-355-1

First Reprint Edition: 2003
(With the permisson of Author)

Published by *Abdul Naeem* for
ISLAMIC BOOK SERVICE
2241, Kucha Chelan, Darya Ganj, New Delhi-110 002
Ph.: 3253514, 3265380, 3286551, Fax: 3277913
e-mail: ibsdelhi@del2.vsnl.net.in
       ibsdelhi@mantraonline.com
       islamic@eth.net
website: http//www.islamic-india.com

Our Associates

I.B.S. Inc.
136, Charlotte Ave., Hicksville, N.Y. 11801.
Ph.: 516-870-0427, Fax: 516-870-0429,
Toll Free # 866-242-4IBS
E-mail: sales@islamicbookservices.com
      ibsny@conversent.net

Al Munna Book Shop Ltd.
P.O. Box-3449, **Sharjah** (U.A.E.), Tel.: 06-561-5483, 06-561-4650
E-mail: nusrat@emirates.net.ae
Dubai Branch: Tel.: 04-352-9294

Printed at: *Noida Printing Press,* C-31, Sector-7, Noida (Ghaziabad) U.P.

Contents

PREFACE TO THE THIRD EDITION

A little over a year has passed since the second edition of this book was published, and, by God's grace, copies are no longer available for distribution. However, the public demand for the book has progressively increased, especially since its disappearance from the book stores. My impressions concerning the need throughout the Muslim world for the clarifications and recommendations contained in the text have proven true. Not merely because the book has been a relative commercial success, but because of the very positive intellectual response which I have received from those who had read it. In fact, in order to make the information contained in the text available to an even wider audience, some readers have already undertaken a Tamil translation of the book, and an Urdu translation has also been commissioned. Consequently, I felt obliged to reprint the book, in order to increase the circulation of its contents among English readers and to meet the growing commercial demand for the book.

Due to technical problems faced in the first edition which caused the print on some of the pages to be faded, I decided to re-typeset the whole text. This also gave me an opportunity to apply the transliteration scheme more carefully throughout the text than in the first edition. I also changed the title of the book from *Evolution of the Madh-habs* to *The Evolution of Fiqh (Islamic Law & The Madh-habs)* in order to further clarify the subject matter of the book. With the exception of chapter one **(The First Stage),** which has been almost totally rewritten, only a few changes have been made within the text itself: corrections where necessary and improvements where possible. However, with regards to the footnotes, there have been quite a few modifications. All the *Hadeeths* mentioned in the text have been thoroughly referenced to existing English translations, with the help of brother Iftekhar Mackeen. As for those *Hadeeths* mentioned in the book which are not found in *Saheeh al-Bukhaaree* or *Saheeh Muslim,* I have endeavored to have them all authenticated in order to remove any doubts in the reader's mind as to their reliability and the conclusions based on them. Likewise, *Hadeeths* which were alluded to in the text have been quoted in the footnotes and or referenced. There have also been some cosmetic changes, like the improved cover design and the reduction of the size of the book, all of which I hope will make this edition somewhat more attractive than its predecessor.

In closing, I ask Almighty Allaah to bless this effort by making it reach those who may most benefit from it, and by adding it to my scale of good deeds on the Day of Judgement.

Abu Ameenah Bilal Philips
Riyadh, August 23rd, 1990

PREFACE TO THE SECOND EDITION

The overall purpose of this book is to acquaint the reader with the historical factors behind the formulation of Islamic law *(Fiqh)*, in order that he or she may better understand how and why the various schools of Islamic law *(Madh-habs)*[1] came about. It is hoped that this understanding will in turn, provide a basis for overcoming the petty differences and divisions which occur when present-day followers of different schools or people without definite schools try to work together. Thus, another aim of this book is to provide a theoretical framework for the reunification of the *Madh-habs* and an ideological basis for Islamic community work free from the divisive effects of *Madh-hab* factionalism.

The pressing need for this book can easily be seen in the dilemma of convert Muslims. In the course of being educated in the basic laws of Islaam, a convert Muslim is gradually presented with a body of laws based on one of the four canonical schools. At the same time he may be informed that there are three other canonical schools, and that all four schools are divinely ordained and infallible. At first this presents no problem for the convert Muslim, since he merely follows the laws presented by his particular teacher, who of course follows one particular *Madh-hab*. When however, the new Muslim convert establishes contact with other Muslims from various parts of the Islamic world, he invariably becomes aware of certain differences in some of the Islamic laws as taught by one or another of the *Madh-habs*. His teacher, a Muslim born into the faith, will no doubt assure him that all four

---

[1] *Madh-hab* is derived from the verb *Dhahaba* which means to go. *Madh-hab* literally means a way of going or simply a path. The position of an outstanding scholar on a particular point was also referred to as his *Madh-hab* (the path of his ideas or his opinion). Eventually, it was used to refer to the sum total of a scholar's opinions, whether legal or philosophical. Later it was used to denote, not only the scholar's opinion, but also that of his students and followers.

Madh-habs are correct in themselves and that so long as he follows one of them he is on the right path. However, some of the differences from one school to another are perplexing for the new Muslim convert. For example, common sense tells him that one cannot be in a state of *Wudoo*[1] while being out of it at the same time. But according to one *Madh-hab*, certain acts break *Wudoo*, while according to another *Madh-hab* those same acts do not[2]. How can a given act be both allowable (*Halaal*) and forbidden (*Haraam*) at the same time. This contradiction has also become apparent to thinking Muslims, young and old, who are concerned about the prevailing stagnation and decline in the Muslim world and who are advocating the revival of Islaam in its original purity and unity.

Faced with several unresolved contradictions, some Muslims have chosen to reject the *Madh-habs* and their rulings, claiming that they will be guided only by the Qur'aan and the Sunnah[3]. Others take the position that despite these contradictions the *Madh-habs* are divinely ordained and therefore one need only choose one of them and follow it without question. Both of these outcomes are undesirable. The latter perpetuates that sectarianism which split the ranks of Muslims in the past and which continues to do so today. The former position of rejecting the *Madh-habs* in their entirety, and consequently the *Fiqh* of earlier generations, leads inevitably to extremism and deviation when those who rely exclusively on the Qur'aan and the Sunnah attempt to apply *Sharee'ah* law to new situations which were not specifically ruled on in either the Qur'aan or the Sunnah. Clearly, both of these outcomes are serious threats to the solidarity and purity of Islaam. As the Prophet (ﷺ) stated, *"The best generation is my gen-*

---

[1] Usually translated as ablution it refers to a ritual state of purity stipulated as a precondition for certain acts of worship.

[2] See pages 76-7 of this book.

[3] The way of life of the Prophet (ﷺ). His sayings, actions and silent approvals which were of legislative value. As a body they represent the second most important source of Islamic law.

eration and then those who follow them[1]. If we accept the divinely inspired wisdom of the Prophet (ﷺ), it follows that the farther we go from the Prophet's (ﷺ) generation, the less likely we are to be able to interpret correctly and apply the real intentions implied in the Qur'aan and the Sunnah. An equally obvious deduction is the fact that the rulings of older scholars of note are more likely to represent the true intentions deducible from the Qur'aan and the Sunnah. These older rulings - the basis of *Fiqh* - are therefore important links and guidelines which cannot wisely be ignored in our study and continued application of Allaah's laws. It stands to reason that our knowledge and correct application of these laws depend upon a sound knowledge of the evolution of *Fiqh* over the ages. Similarly, a study of this development automatically embraces a study of the evolution of the *Madh-habs* and their important contributions to *Fiqh*, as well as the reasons for apparent contradictions in some of their rulings.

Armed with this background knowledge, the thinking Muslim, be he new convert or born into the faith, will be in a position to understand the source of those perplexing contradictions and to place them in their new proper perspective. Hopefully, he will then join the ranks of those who would work actively for the re-establishment of unity *(Tawheed)*, not only as the mainspring of our belief in Allaah, but also in relation to the *Madh-habs* and to the practical application of the laws which underlie and shape the way of life known as Islaam.

The basic material for this book was taken from my class notes and research papers for a graduate course on the history of Islamic legislation *(Taareekh at-Tashree')* taught by Dr. 'Assaal at the University of Riyadh. The material was translated into English, further developed and utilized as teaching material for a grade twelve Islamic Education class which I taught at Manaret ar-Riyadh private school in 1980-81. This teaching text was published in the spring of 1982 by As-Suq

---

[1] Narrated by 'Imraan ibn Husain and collected by al-Bukhaaree (Muhammed Muhsin Khan, *Sahih Al-Bukhari*, (Arabic-English), (Madeenah: Islamic University, 2nd ed., 1976), vol. 5, p. 2, no. 3.

Bookstore, Brooklyn, New York, under the title, *Lessons in Fiqh*. The present work is a revised and expanded edition of *Lessons in Fiqh*.

I would like to thank sister Jameelah Jones for patiently typing and proofreading the manuscript, and my father, Bradley Earle Philips, for his suggestions and careful editing of the text.

It is hoped that this book on the history of *Fiqh* will help the reader to place the *Madh-habs* in proper perspective and to appreciate the pressing need for their re-unification.

In closing, I pray that Allaah, the Supreme, accept this minor effort toward the clarification of His chosen religion, Islaam, as it is His acceptance alone which ultimately counts.

Was-Salaam 'Alaykum,
Abu Ameenah Bilaal Philips
25th Nov. 1983 / 21st Safar 1404

TRANSLITERATION

Arabic	English	Arabic	English
أ	a	ل	l
ب	b	م	m
ت	t	ن	n
ث	th	ه	h
ج	j	ة	h/t[1]
ح	ḥ	و	w
خ	kh	ي	y
د	d		
ذ	dh	**VOWELS**	
ر	r	**Short Vowels**	
ز	z	َ	a
س	s	ِ	i
ش	sh	ُ	u
ص	ṣ	**Long Vowels**	
ض	ḍ	ا ـ آ	aa
ط	ṭ	ـِي	ee
ظ	dH	ـُو	oo
ع	'	**Dipthongs**	
غ	gh	ـَو	aw
ف	f	ـَي	ay
ق	q		
ك	k		

---

[1] This *taa* has been commonly transliterated as "t" in all cases. However, such a system is not accurate and does not represent Arabic pronunciation.

In order to provide the non-Arab with a more easily read set of symbols than those in current use, I have adopted a somewhat innovative system of transliteration particularly with regard to long vowels. It should be noted, however, that a very similar system was used by E.W. Lane in preparing his famous *Arabic-English Lexicon,* considered the most authoritative work in its field. Many other scholarly texts, written to teach Arabic pronunciation, also use similar systems. For example, Margaret K. Omar's *Saudi Arabic: Urban Hijazi Dialect,* (Washington, DC; Foreign Service Institute, 1975), as well as the Foreign Language Institute's *Saudi-Arabic: Headstart* (Monetery, CA: Defense Language Institute, 1980).

No transliteration can express exactly the vocalic differences between two languages nor can Roman characters give anything more than an approximate sound of the original Arabic words and phrases. There is also the difficulty of romanizing certain combinations of Arabic words which are pronounced differently from the written characters. Included in this category is the prefix *"al"* (representing the article "the"). When it precedes words beginning with letters known as *al-Ḥuroof ash-Shamseeyah* (lit. solar letters), the sound of *"l"* is merged into the following letter; for example, *al-Raḥmaan* is pronounced *ar-Raḥmaan.* Whereas, in the caşe of all other letters, known as *al-Ḥuroof al-Qamareeyah* (lit. lunar letters), the *"al"* is pronounced fully. I have followed the pronunciation for the facility of the average reader by writing *ar-Raḥmaan* instead of *al-Raḥmaan* and so on.

Note:

Shaddah (ّ) The *Shaddah* is represented in Roman letters by doubled consonants. However, in actual pronunciation the letters should be merged and held briefly like the "n" sound produced by the *n/kn* combination in the word *unknown,* or the "n" in *unnerve,* the "b" in *grabbag,* the "t" in *freight-train,* the "r" in *overruled,* and "p" in *lamp post,* and the "d" in *mid-day.*

I have made an exception with (ـِيّ), instead of *iyy,* I have used *eey* as in *Islaameeyah* because this more accurately conveys the sound.

INTRODUCTION

Fiqh and *Sharee'ah*

For a proper understanding of the historical development of Islamic law, the terms *Fiqh* and *Sharee'ah* need to be defined. *Fiqh* has been loosely translated into English as *"Islamic law"* and so has *Sharee'ah*, but these terms are not synonymous either in the Arabic language or to the Muslim scholar.

Fiqh literally means, the true understanding of what is intended. An example of this usage can be found in the Prophet Muhammad's statement: *"To whomsoever Allaah wishes good, He gives the Fiqh (true understanding) of the Religion"*[1]. Technically, however, *Fiqh* refers to **the science of deducing Islamic laws from evidence found in the sources of Islamic law.** By extension it also means the body of Islamic laws so deduced.

Sharee'ah, literally means, *a waterhole* where animals gather daily to drink, or the *straight path* as in the Qur'anic verse,

ثُمَّ جَعَلْنَٰكَ عَلَىٰ شَرِيعَةٖ مِّنَ ٱلۡأَمۡرِ فَٱتَّبِعۡهَا وَلَا تَتَّبِعۡ أَهۡوَآءَ ٱلَّذِينَ لَا يَعۡلَمُونَ

"Then We put you on a straight path *(Sharee'ah)* in your affairs, so follow it and do not follow the desires of those who have no knowledge."[2]

Islamically, however it refers to the sum total of Islamic laws which were revealed to the Prophet Muhammad (ﷺ), and which are recorded in the Qur'aan as well as deducible from the Prophet's

---

[1] Reported by Mu'aawiyah and collected by al-Bukhaaree *(Sahih Al-Bukhari* (Arabic-English), vol. 4, pp. 223-4, no. 346), Muslim, (Abdul Hamid Siddiqi, *Sahih Muslim* (English Trans.), (Beirut: Dar al-Arabia, n.d.), vol. 3, p. 1061, no. 4720), at-Tirmidhee and others.

[2] Soorah al-Jaathiyah (45):18.

divinely-guided lifestyle (called the *Sunnah*).[1]

The Distinction

From the previous two definitions, the following three differences may be deduced:

1. *Sharee'ah* is the body of revealed laws found both in the Qur'aan and in the Sunnah, while *Fiqh* is a body of laws deduced from *Sharee'ah* to cover specific situations not directly treated in *Sharee'ah law*.

2. *Sharee'ah* is fixed and unchangeable, whereas *Fiqh* changes according to the circumstances under which it is applied.

3. The laws of *Sharee'ah* are, for the most part, general: they lay down basic principles. In contrast, the laws of *Fiqh* tend to be specific: they demonstrate how the basic principles of *Sharee'ah* should be applied in given circumstances.

Note

1. In this book on the evolution of *Fiqh* the term *"Islamic Law"* will be used to mean the laws of *Sharee'ah* and the laws of *Fiqh* combined. The terms *Fiqh* or *Laws of Fiqh* and *Sharee'ah* or *Laws of Sharee'ah* will be used where a distinction seems necessary.

2. At the end of this book there is a glossary of Arabic terms and their plurals used in this book. In the text of this book the English plural is used except in cases where the Arabic plural is more widely known. For example, Muslims is used instead of *Muslimoon* and *Soorahs* instead of *Suwar*.

The Development of *Fiqh*

The development of *Fiqh*, falls traditionally into six major stages named as follows: **foundation, Establishment, Building, Flowering, Consolidation,** and **Stagnation and Decline.**

---

[1] Muhammad Shalabee, *al-Madkhal fee at-Ta'reef bil-Fiqh al-Islaamee*, (Beirut: Daar an-Nahdah al-Arabeeyah, 1969), p. 28.

These stages occur respectively in the following historical periods:

(a) **Foundation** : the era of the Prophet (ﷺ) (609-632 CE)[1]

(b) **Establishment** : the era of the Righteous Caliphs, from the death of the Prophet (ﷺ) to the middle of the seventh century CE (632-661)

(c) **Building** : from the founding of the Umayyad dynasty (661 CE) until its decline in the middle of the 8th century CE.

(d) **Flowering** : from the rise of the 'Abbaasid dynasty in the middle of the 8th century CE to the beginning of its decline around the middle of the 10th century CE.

(e) **Consolidation** : the decline of the 'Abbaasid dynasty from about 960 CE to the murder of the last 'Abbaasid Caliph at the hands of the Mongols in the middle of the 13th century CE.

(f) **Stagnation and Decline** : from the sacking of Baghdad in 1258 CE to the present.

---

[1] C.E. (i.e. Christian Era) is used instead of A.D. (Anno Domini, lit. in the year of our Lord) because Muslims do not recognize Jesus the son of Mary as the Lord, but as a Prophet of God.

In this work the above mentioned stages in the development of *Fiqh* will be described with special reference to the relevant social and political context of the respective periods. As the reader follows this development, he will be given insight into the evolution of the *Madh-habs* (schools of Islamic legal thought) as well as their contributions to *Fiqh*. Hopefully he will then be able to appreciate the fact that all the *Madh-habs* have contributed in different degrees to the development of *Fiqh*, and that no single *Madh-hab* can properly be claimed to represent Islaam or Islamic law in its totality. In other words, *Fiqh* is not determined by any one school of thought acting alone. All *Madh-habs* have been important instruments for the clarification and application of the *Sharee'ah*. Together, *Fiqh* and *Sharee'ah* should be unifying forces that unite all Muslims regardless of place, time or cultural background. In fact, the only infallible *Madh-hab* which deserves to be followed without any questions asked is that of the Prophet Muhammad himself (🕌). Only his interpretations of *Sharee'ah* can be considered divinely guided and meant to be followed until the last day of this world. All other *Madh-habs* are the result of human effort, and thus are subject to human error. Or as Imaam ash-Shaafi'ee, founder of the Shaafi'ee *Madh-hab*, so wisely put it, *"There isn't any of us who hasn't had a saying or action of Allaah's messenger (🕌) elude him or slip his mind. So no matter what rulings I have made or fundamental principles I have established, there will be in them things contrary to the way of Allaah's messenger (🕌). However, the correct ruling is according to what the messenger of Allaah (🕌) said, and that is my true ruling."*[1]

---

[1] Collected by al-Haakim with a continuous chain of reliable narrators to ash-Shaafi'ee (Ibn 'Asaakir, *Taareekh Dimishq*, vol. 15, sec. 1, p. 3 and Ibn Qayyim, *I'laam al-Mooqi'een*, (Egypt: Al-Haajj 'Abdus-Salaam Press, 1968), vol. 2, p. 363).

1. THE FIRST STAGE: FOUNDATION

The first stage in the development of *Fiqh* covers the era of the Prophet Muhammad ibn 'Abdillaah's apostleship (609-632 C.E.) during which the only source of Islamic law was divine revelation in the form of either the Qur'aan or the *Sunnah* [the sayings and actions of the Prophet (鑿)]. The Qur'aan represented the blueprint for the Islamic way of life, and the Prophet's application of the blueprint in his day-to-day life (i.e. the *Sunnah)* acted as a detailed explanation of the general principles outlined in the Qur'aan, as well as a practical demonstration of their application.[1]

The Method of Legislation

Sections of the Qur'aan were continuously revealed to the Prophet Muhammad (鑿) from the beginning of his prohethood in the year 609 C.E. until shortly before his death (632 C.E.), a period of approximately twenty-three years. The various sections of the Qur'aan were generally revealed to solve the problems which confronted the Prophet (鑿) and his followers in both Makkah and Madeenah. A number of Qur'anic verses are direct answers to questions raised by Muslims as well as non-Muslims during the era of prophethood. Many of these verses actually begin with the phrase "They ask you about.." For example.

يَسْـَٔلُونَكَ عَنِ ٱلشَّهْرِ ٱلْحَرَامِ قِتَالٍ فِيهِ قُلْ قِتَالٌ فِيهِ كَبِيرٌ وَصَدٌّ عَن سَبِيلِ ٱللَّهِ وَكُفْرٌ بِهِۦ وَٱلْمَسْجِدِ ٱلْحَرَامِ وَإِخْرَاجُ أَهْلِهِۦ مِنْهُ أَكْبَرُ عِندَ ٱللَّهِ

"They ask you about fighting in the forbidden months. Say, 'Fighting in them is a grave offense, but blocking Allaah's path and denying Him is even graver in Allaah's sight.' "[2]

---

[1] *al-Madkhal*, p. 50.

[2] Soorah al-Baqarah (2):217.

$$\text{يَسْتَلُونَكَ عَنِ الْخَمْرِ وَالْمَيْسِرِ قُلْ فِيهِمَآ إِثْمٌ كَبِيرٌ وَمَنَافِعُ لِلنَّاسِ وَإِثْمُهُمَآ أَكْبَرُ مِن نَّفْعِهِمَا}$$

"They ask you about wine and gambling. Say, 'There is great evil in them as well as benefit to man. But the evil is greater than the benefit.' "[1]

$$\text{وَيَسْتَلُونَكَ عَنِ الْمَحِيضِ قُلْ هُوَ أَذًى فَاعْتَزِلُوا النِّسَاءَ فِي الْمَحِيضِ}$$

"They ask you about menses. Say, 'It is harm, so stay away from (sexual relations with) women during their menses.' "[2]

A number of other verses were revealed due to particular incidents which took place during the era of the Prophet (ﷺ). An example can be found in the case of Hilaal ibn Umayyah who came before the Prophet (ﷺ) and accused his wife of adultery with another of the Prophet's companions. The Prophet (ﷺ) said, *"Either you bring proof (i.e., three other witnesses) or you will receive the fixed punishment (of eighty lashes) on your back."* Hilaal said, "Oh Messenger of Allaah! If any of us saw a man on top of his wife, would he go looking for witnesses?" However, the Prophet (ﷺ) repeated his demand for proof. Then angel Gabriel came and revealed to the Prophet (ﷺ) the verse:[3]

$$\text{وَالَّذِينَ يَرْمُونَ أَزْوَاجَهُمْ وَلَمْ يَكُن لَّهُمْ شُهَدَاءُ إِلَّا أَنفُسُهُمْ فَشَهَادَةُ أَحَدِهِمْ أَرْبَعُ شَهَادَاتٍ بِاللَّهِ إِنَّهُ لَمِنَ الصَّادِقِينَ ۝ وَالْخَامِسَةُ أَنَّ لَعْنَتَ اللَّهِ}$$

---

[1] Soorah al-Baqarah (2): 219.

[2] Soorah al-Baqarah (2):222.

[3] Collected by al-Bukhaaree *(Sahih Al-Bukhari (Arabic-English),* vol. 6, pp. 245-6, no. 271).

عَلَيْهِ إِن كَانَ مِنَ ٱلْكَٰذِبِينَ ۝ وَيَدْرَؤُا۟ عَنْهَا ٱلْعَذَابَ أَن تَشْهَدَ أَرْبَعَ شَهَٰدَٰتٍ بِٱللَّهِ إِنَّهُۥ لَمِنَ ٱلْكَٰذِبِينَ ۝ وَٱلْخَٰمِسَةَ أَنَّ غَضَبَ ٱللَّهِ عَلَيْهَآ إِن كَانَ مِنَ ٱلصَّٰدِقِينَ ۝

"As for those who accuse their wives and have no evidence but their own, their witness can be four declarations with oaths by Allaah that they are truthful and a fifth invoking Allaah's curse on themselves if they are lying. But the punishment will be averted from the wife if she bears witness four times with oaths by Allaah that he is lying, and a fifth oath invoking Allaah's curse on herself if he is telling the truth."[1]

The same was the case of Islamic legislation found in the *Sunnah,* much of which was either the result of answers to questions, or were pronouncements made at the time that incidents took place. For example, on one occasion, one of the Prophet's companions asked him, *"Oh Messenger of Allaah! We sail the seas and if we make Wudoo (ablutions) with our fresh water we will go thirsty. Can we make Wudoo with sea water?"* He replied, *"Its water is pure and its dead (sea creatures) are Halaal (permissible to eat)."*[2]

The reason for this method of legislation was to achieve gradation in the enactment of laws, as this approach was more easily acceptable by Arabs who were used to complete freedom. It also made it easier for them to learn and understand the laws since the reasons and context of the legislation would be known to them. This method of gradual legislation was not limited to the laws as a whole, but it also took place dur-

---

[1] Soorah an-Noor (24):6-9.

[2] Collected by at-Tirmidhee, an-Nasaa'ee, Ibn Maajah and Abu Daawood *(Sunan Abu Dawud* (English Trans.), p. 22, no. 38), an authenticated by al-Albaanee in *Saheeh Sunan Abee Daawood,* (Beirut: al-Maktab al-Islaamee, 1st ed., 1988), vol. 1, p. 19, no. 76.

ing the enactment of a number of individual laws. The legislation of *Salaah* (formal prayers) is a good example of gradation in the enactment of individual laws. In the early Makkan period, *Salaah* was initially twice per day, once in the morning and once at night.[1] Shortly before the migration to Madeenah, five times daily *Salaah* was enjoined on the believers. However, *Salaah* at that time consisted of only two units per prayer, with the exception of Maghrib (sunset) prayers which were three units. After the early Muslims had become accustomed to regular prayer, the number of units were increased to four for residents, except for Fajr (early morning) prayer and that of Maghrib.[2]

General Content of the Qur'aan

In Makkah, Muslims were an oppressed minority, whereas after their migration to Madeenah they became the ruling majority. Thus, the revelations of the Qur'aan during the two phases had unique characteristics which distinguished them from each other.

The Makkan Period (609-622 C.E.)

This period starts with the beginning of the prophethood in Makkah and ends with the Prophet's *Hijrah* (migration) to the city of Madeenah. The revelations of this period were mainly concerned with building the ideological foundation of Islaam, *Eemaan* (faith), in order to prepare the early band of converts for the difficult task of practically establishing the social order of Islaam. Consequently, the following basic topics of the Makkan revelations all reflect one aspect or another of principles designed to build faith in God.

(i) Tawheed (Allaah's Unity)

Most of the people of Makkah believed in a Supreme Being known by the name "Allaah" from the most ancient of times. However, they had added a host of gods who shared some of Allaah's powers or acted as intermediaries. Accordingly, Makkan revelations

---

[1] *al-Madkhal*, p. 74-8.

[2] See *Sahih Al-Bukhari* (Arabic-English), vol. 1, p. 214, no. 346.

declared Allaah's unique unity and pointed out that gods besides Allaah are of no benefit.

(ii) Allaah's Existence
Some of the early verses presented logical arguments proving the existence of God for the few Makkans who actually denied it.

(iii) The Next Life
Since there was no way for human beings to know about the next life, the Makkan revelations vividly described its wonders, its mysteries and its horrors.

(iv) The People of Old
The Makkan verses often mentioned historical examples of earlier civilizations which were destroyed when they denied their obligation to God, like the 'Aad and the Thamood, in order to warn those who rejected the message of Islaam and to teach the believers about the greatness of Allaah.

(v) Salaah (Formal Prayer)
Because of the critical relationship between *Salaah* and *Tawheed*, *Salaah* was the only other pillar of Islaam to be legislated in Makkah, besides the declaration of faith *(Tawheed)*.

(vi) Challenges
In order to prove to the pagan Makkans that the Qur'aan was from God, some of the Makkan verses challenged the Arabs to imitiate the style of the Qur'aan.[1]

The Madeenan Period (622-632 C.E.)

The *Hijrah* marks the beginning of this period and the death of the Prophet (ﷺ) in 632 C.E. marks the end. After the Prophet's migration to Madeenah and the spread of Islaam there, he was appointed as the ruler, and the Muslim community became a fledgling state. Thus, revelation was concerned primarily with the organization of the Muslim state. And it was during this period that the majority of the social

---

[1] *al-Madkhal,* 51-5.

and economic laws of the *Sharee'ah* were revealed. Revelations during this period also strengthened the foundations of *Eemaan* and *Tawheed* which were established during the Makkan period. However, most of the following basic topics of the Madeenan revelations concentrate on the laws necessary for the development of an Islamic nation.

(i) Laws

It was during the Madeenan period that the last three pillars of Islaam were revealed, as well as the prohibition of intoxicants, pork, gambling, and the punishments for adultery, murder and theft were fixed.

(ii) Jihaad

During the Makkan period, Muslim were forbidden to take up arms against the Makkans who were oppressing them, in order to avoid their decimation and to develop their patience. The right to fight against the enemy as well as the rules of war were revealed in Madeenah after the numbers of Muslims had dramatically increased.

(iii) People of the Book

In Madeenah, Muslims came in contact with Jews for the first time and with Christians on a large scale. Thus, a number of Madeenan verses tackled questions which were raised by the Jews in order to befuddle the Prophet (ﷺ) and discredit Islaam. The verses also outlined laws concerning political alliances with Christians and Jews, as well as laws permitting marriage with them.

(iv) The Munaafiqs (Hypocrites)

For the first time since the beginning of the final message, people began to enter the fold of Islaam without really believing in it. Some entered Islaam to try to destroy it from within because Muslims were strong and they could not openly oppose them, while others entered and exited shortly thereafter in order to shake the faith of the believers. Consequently, some Madeenan verses exposed their plots and warned against them, while others laid the foundations for the laws concerning apostates. [1]

Qur'anic Fields of Study.

The body of information contained in the Qur'aan, as a whole, may be grouped under three general headings with regards to the fields of study to which they are related:

First: Information related to Belief in God, His angels, His scriptures His prophets, and the affairs of the next life. These topics are covered within the field of study known as theology *('Ilm al-Kalaam* or *al-'Aqeedah).*

Second: Information related to deeds of the heart and soul, and moral principles and rules of conduct aimed at the development of nobility of character. These areas represent the field of moral science known as ethics *('Ilm al-Akhlaaq).*

Third: Information related to deeds of the limbs and contained within a body of commandments, prohibitions and choices. This group represents the field of law. [2]

Legal Content of the Qur'aan

Islamic legislation in the Qur'aan is comprised of a variety of acts which have been enjoined by divine decree on mankind. These acts may be grouped in two basic categories with regard to the parties involved in the acts:

A. Dealings between Allaah and man. These are the religious rites which are not valid without correct intentions. Some of them are purely religious forms of worship, like prayer and fasting; while others are socio-economic forms of worship, like *Zakaah* (compulsory charity); and yet others are socio-physical forms of worship, like *Hajj* (pil-

---

[1] Mannaa' al-Qattaan, *Mabaahith fee 'Uloom al-Qur'aan*, (Riyadh: Maktab al-Ma'aarif, 8th printing, 1981), pp. 63-4, and *al-Madkhal*, pp. 55-7.

[2] Muhammad al-Khidaree Bek, *Taareekh at-Tashree' al-Islaamee*, (Cairo: al-Maktabah at-Tijaareeyah al-Kubraa, 1960). pp. 17-8.

grimage to Makkah). These four acts of worship are considered the foundation of Islaam after faith *(Eemaan).*

B. Dealings among men. The laws governing these dealings may themselves be divided into four sub-sections relative to the subject matter of the dealings:

a) Laws ensuring and defending the propagation of Islaam. These, are embodied in the códes of armed or unarmed struggle *(Jihaad).*

b) Family laws for the development and protection of the family structure. These include laws concerning marriage, divorce and inheritance.

c) Trade laws governing business transactions, rental contracts, etc.

d) Criminal laws specifying punishments and or compensations for various crimes. [1]

The Basis of Legislation in the Qur'aan

The Qur'aan itself announces that it was revealed to reform human conditions. Islaam did not erase all pre-Islamic customs and practises. Instead, it removed every facet of corruption and cancelled all customs which were harmful to the society. Consequently, Islamic legislation forbade interest because it takes unfair advantage of the less fortunate members of society; fornication was forbidden due to its exploitation of women and the destruction of family bonds; and alcohol was prohibited because of the physical, psychological and spiritual damage which it inflicts on both the individual and society as a whole. Trade practices were reformed by making the basis of trade mutual consent, and by disallowing all deceptive business transactions. The existing system of marriage was organized by confirming certain forms and prohibiting others which were, in fact, fornication or something close

---

[1] *Taareekh at-Tashree' al-Islaamee,* pp. 34-5.

to it. The basis of divorce was also recognized, but its pronouncements were limited.

Because Islaam did not come to destroy human civilization, morals and customs, in order to build on it a new civilization with new morals and customs, it looked at everything from the perspective of human welfare; what was harmful was removed and what was beneficial was confirmed. Allaah says in the Qur'aan:

$$ يَأْمُرُهُم بِٱلْمَعْرُوفِ وَيَنْهَىٰهُمْ عَنِ ٱلْمُنكَرِ وَيُحِلُّ لَهُمُ ٱلطَّيِّبَـٰتِ وَيُحَرِّمُ عَلَيْهِمُ ٱلْخَبَـٰٓئِثَ $$

"It commands them to do righteousness and prohibits them from evil, and it makes allowable to them the good things and makes forbidden to them all filth." [1]

Islaam is fundamentally a system of building and not one of destruction as its goal is reformation and not merely control and government. It should be noted, however, that Islaam's confirmation of some Arab customs does not mean that it has taken its laws and principles from other sources, nor does it mean that those practises which it confirmed are not a part of divine law. Whatever Islaam confirmed is considered an integral part of the divine code for the following reasons:

a) Some of the practises were inherited from earlier generations to whom prophets had been sent. A good example of this is *Hajj* which was instituted by Prophet Abraham and Ishmael.

b) Islamic principles do not contradict human reason nor are they unintelligible. Instead, they free the human intellect from irrationality. Consequently, they recognize the useful results of human intellectual activity.

c) If the confirmed practises were not present, Islaam would have instituted them due to the existing human need for them.

---

[1] Soorah al-A'raaf (7):157.

Nevertheless, the number of confirmed practices were, in fact, quite few in proportion to the many which were cancelled. And, furthermore, even the little that was confirmed was not kept in its existing form. Only its foundation remained untouched.[1]

In order for Islamic legislation to achieve its goal of reformation, it has enacted a series of legal commandments and prohibitions which make up the rules of conduct governing the social system of Islaam. However, in the enactment of laws, the Qur'anic revelations have taken into consideration the following four basic principles:

1. The Removal of Difficulty.

The system of Islaam has been revealed for man's benefit. It provides him with guidance in all walks of life in order to ensure for him a righteous lifestyle within a just society committed to the service of God. Islamic laws are not meant to be a burden, creating difficulties for man in order for him to grow spiritually, as some systems may claim. They are designed to facilitate mankind's individual and societal needs. As such, among the pillars on which Islaam is based is the removal of unnecessary difficulties wherever possible. Evidence to support the fact that Islamic law is based on the concept of removal of difficulty can be found throughout the Qur'aan. The following verses from the Qur'aan are only a few examples:

لَا يُكَلِّفُ ٱللَّهُ نَفْسًا إِلَّا وُسْعَهَا

"Allaah does not burden a soul with more than it can bear."[2]

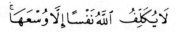

"Allaah wishes for you ease and He does not wish difficulty for you."[3]

---

[1] *al-Madkhal*, pp. 57-9.

[2] Soorah al-Baqarah (2):286.

[3] Soorah al-Baqarah (2):185.

$$\text{وَمَاجَعَلَ عَلَيْكُمْ فِى ٱلدِّينِ مِنْ حَرَجٍ}$$

"He did not make any difficulty for you in the religion." [1]

$$\text{يُرِيدُ ٱللَّهُ أَن يُخَفِّفَ عَنكُمْ وَخُلِقَ ٱلْإِنسَـٰنُ ضَعِيفًا}$$

"Allaah wishes to lighten the burden for you, for man was created weak." [2]

Because of this principle, Allaah has enacted along with the divine laws a variety of legal concessions, like the permission to break fast, and shorten and join prayers during travel. Moreover, the consumption of prohibited substances (e.g., pork and alcohol) in cases of dire necessity was also permitted.

$$\text{فَمَنِ ٱضْطُرَّ فِى مَخْمَصَةٍ غَيْرَ مُتَجَانِفٍ لِّإِثْمٍ فَإِنَّ ٱللَّهَ غَفُورٌ رَّحِيمٌ}$$

"But if anyone is forced by hunger, with no inclination to transgression, Allaah is indeed Oft-forgiving, Most Merciful." [3]

The Prophet (ﷺ), who was the prime example of how Islamic law was to be implemented, was himself described as always choosing the easier path whenever a choice was given to him between two possible paths, as long as the easier path was not sinful. [4] He was also reported to have said to some of his followers on the occasion of their dispatchment as governors of Yemen, *"Make things easy (for the people) and*

---

[1] Soorah al- Hajj (22):78.

[2] Soorah an-Nisaa (4):28.

[3] Soorah al-Maa'idah (5):4.

[4] Reported by 'Aa'eshah and collected by al-Bukhaaree *(Sahih Al-Bukhari* (Arabic-English), vol. 4, p. 491, no. 760), Muslim *(Sahih Muslim* (English Trans.), vol. 4, p. 1246, no. 5752) and Abu Daawood *(Sunan Abu Dawud* (English Trans.), vol. 3, p. 1341, no. 4767).

do not make them difficult." [1]

Islamic legal scholars unanimously consider this concept an indisputable fundamental principle followed by God in the enactment of laws. Consequently, in their implementation of the divine laws, they have deduced many secondary laws on this basis. [2]

2. The Reduction of Religious Obligations.

A natural consequence of the previous principle is that the total number of legal obligations should be relatively few. Accordingly , the prohibited acts and substances in Islamic legislation are quite few in comparison to those which are allowed by direct command or by the absence of any command or prohibition. This principle can be clearly seen in the method by which the Qur'aan deals with prohibitions and permissions. In the case of prohibitions, the sub-categories are named and listed, while in the case of permissions, a general allowance is given due to the great number of categories included in it. For example, with regard to women with whom marriage is forbidden, Allaah states,

حُرِّمَتْ عَلَيْكُمْ أُمَّهَٰتُكُمْ وَبَنَاتُكُمْ وَأَخَوَٰتُكُمْ وَعَمَّٰتُكُمْ

"Prohibited to you are your mothers, your daughters, your sisters and your aunts..." [3]

After completing the prohibited categories, Allaah says,

وَأُحِلَّ لَكُم مَّا وَرَآءَ ذَٰلِكُمْ أَن تَبْتَغُوا بِأَمْوَٰلِكُم مُّحْصِنِينَ غَيْرَ مُسَٰفِحِينَ

---

[1] Reported by Abu Burdah and collected by al-Bukhaaree *(Sahih Al-Bukhari* (Arabic-English), vol. 5, pp. 441-3, no. 630), and Muslim *(Sahih Muslim* (English Trans.), vol. 3, p. 944, no. 4298). Muslim also collected it from Abu Moosaa (no. 4297) and Anas ibn Maalik (no. 4300).

[2] *Taareekh at-Tashree' al-Islaamee*, pp. 19-20 and *al-Madkhal*, pp. 85-89.

[3] Soorah an-Nisaa (4):23.

"Except for these, all others are lawful, provided you seek them in marriage with a dowry and not for fornication."[1]

As for foods, the forbidden categories are also listed in detail. The Qur'aan states,

$$حُرِّمَتْ عَلَيْكُمُ الْمَيْتَةُ وَالدَّمُ وَلَحْمُ الْخِنزِيرِ وَمَآ أُهِلَّ لِغَيْرِ اللهِ بِهِ وَالْمُنْخَنِقَةُ وَالْمَوْقُوذَةُ وَالْمُتَرَدِّيَةُ وَالنَّطِيحَةُ$$

"Forbidden to you (for food) are: animals which die of themselves, blood, pork, animals slaughtered in the name of others besides Allaah, animals killed by strangulation, or a blow, or a fall, or by being gored..."[2]

On the other hand, in regard to the permissible foods, Allaah states,

$$الْيَوْمَ أُحِلَّ لَكُمُ الطَّيِّبَتُ وَطَعَامُ الَّذِينَ أُوتُوا الْكِتَبَ حِلٌّ لَّكُمْ وَطَعَامُكُمْ حِلٌّ لَّهُمْ$$

"On this day all good things are made lawful for you. The food of the people of the Book is lawful to you and your food is lawful to them..."[3]

Furthermore, in spite of the fact that the things which have been forbidden are quite few in comparison to those which have been permitted, the sin of one who is forced to take forbidden substances has also been lifted, as was mentioned previously. Allaah states this concession in a number of places in the Qur'aan. For example:

$$فَمَنِ اضْطُرَّ غَيْرَ بَاغٍ وَلَا عَادٍ فَلَا إِثْمَ عَلَيْهِ إِنَّ اللهَ غَفُورٌ رَّحِيمٌ$$

---

[1] Soorah an-Nisaa (4): 24.

[2] Soorah al-Maa'idah (5):3.

[3] Soorah al-Maa'idah (5):5.

**"But if anyone is forced by necessity, without willful dis-
obedience, nor transgressing due limits, there is no sin on
him. For Allaah is Oft-forgiving, Most Merciful."** [1]

It is also worth noting that the laws, on the whole, do not contain so
many details as to create difficulty for those who wish to strictly follow
the teachings of the Qur'aan. Among the verses of the Qur'aan which
indicate the existence of this principle is the following:

يَـٰٓأَيُّهَا ٱلَّذِينَ ءَامَنُوا۟ لَا تَسْـَٔلُوا۟ عَنْ أَشْيَآءَ إِن تُبْدَ لَكُمْ تَسُؤْكُمْ وَإِن
تَسْـَٔلُوا۟ عَنْهَا حِينَ يُنَزَّلُ ٱلْقُرْءَانُ تُبْدَ لَكُمْ عَفَا ٱللَّهُ عَنْهَا وَٱللَّهُ
غَفُورٌ حَلِيمٌ

**"Oh you who believe, do not ask about things which, if
made plain for you, will cause you trouble. But if you ask
about them while the Qur'aan is being revealed, they will
be made plain to you. Allaah has exempted them. And
Allaah is Oft-Forgiving, Most Gentle."** [2]

The prohibited questions concern issues about which Allaah has
chosen to enact prohibitions due to their questions. And, if they did
not ask about them, they would have been left with a choice between
doing them and not doing them. Included in this category is the
Prophet's (ﷺ) response to a repeated question concerning whether
Hajj was compulsory every year. [3] He said, *"If I said yes, it would have
become compulsory. Leave me alone concerning things which I have
left up to you, for certainly those before you were destroyed because of
their many unnecessary questions and their arguments and disagreements with their prophets."* [4] In another narration, he was reported to

---

[1] Soorah al-Baqarah (2): 173.

[2] Soorah al-Maa'idah (5):104.

[3] *Taareekh at-Tashree' al-Islaamee*, pp. 20-1.

[4] Reported by Abu Hurayrah and collected by Muslim *(Sahih Muslim* (English Trans.), vol. 2, p. 675, no. 3095).

have said, *"If I have prohibited you from doing something, avoid it totally. But, if I command you to do something, do as much of it as you can."* [1] He was also reported to have said, *"The Muslims who have committed the gravest offense against Muslims are those who asked about things which were not prohibited, but which became prohibited because of their questions."* [2]

A good example of limitation of details can be found in the Qur'anic treatment of business transactions. The laws in this regard have not at all been detailed. Instead, general precepts suitable for all circumstances have been legislated. For example, Allaah states:

$$\text{يَٰٓأَيُّهَا ٱلَّذِينَ ءَامَنُوٓا۟ أَوْفُوا۟ بِٱلْعُقُودِ}$$

"Oh you who believe, fulfil your contracts." [3]

$$\text{وَأَحَلَّ ٱللَّهُ ٱلْبَيْعَ وَحَرَّمَ ٱلرِّبَوٰا۟}$$

"Allaah has made trade lawful and prohibited interest." [4]

$$\text{يَٰٓأَيُّهَا ٱلَّذِينَ ءَامَنُوا۟ لَا تَأْكُلُوٓا۟ أَمْوَٰلَكُم بَيْنَكُم بِٱلْبَٰطِلِ إِلَّآ أَن تَكُونَ تِجَٰرَةً عَن تَرَاضٍ مِّنكُمْ}$$

"Oh you who believe, do not eat up your properties amongst yourselves unfairly. But there should be trade by mutual good-will." [5]

---

[1] Reported by Abu Hurayrah and collected by Muslim *(Sahih Muslim* (English Trans.), vol. 4, pp. 1256-7, no. 5818).

[2] Reported by 'Aamir ibn Sa'd and collected by Muslim *(Sahih Muslim* (English Trans.), vol. 4, p. 1257, no. 5821).

[3] Soorah al-Maa'idah (5):1.

[4] Soorah al-Baqarah (2):275.

[5] Soorah an-Nisaa (4):29.

3. The Realization of Public Welfare

Because the laws of Islaam were primarily enacted for the general good of all mankind, the Prophet (ﷺ) was a universal prophet sent to all people till the end of time. Allaah stated that in the Qur'aan in no uncertain terms:

وَمَآ أَرْسَلْنَٰكَ إِلَّا كَآفَّةً لِّلنَّاسِ بَشِيرًا وَنَذِيرًا وَلَٰكِنَّ أَكْثَرَ ٱلنَّاسِ لَا يَعْلَمُونَ

"We have not sent you but as a universal messenger to mankind, giving them glad tidings and warning them (against sin), but most people do not realize it." [1]

قُلْ يَٰٓأَيُّهَا ٱلنَّاسُ إِنِّى رَسُولُ ٱللَّهِ إِلَيْكُمْ جَمِيعًا

"Say, 'Oh mankind, I am the messenger of Allaah to all of you.' " [2]

Naskh (Abrogation)

The existence of abrogation within Islamic legislation is among the manifestations of human welfare considerations in Islamic legislation. God may prescribe a law suitable to people at the time of its enactment, or it may serve a particular limited purpose. However, its suitability may later disappear or its unique purpose may have been achieved. In such circumstances, the need for the law ceases to exist and its validity becomes cancelled. The following are only a few of many such examples which may be found recorded in both the Qur'aan and the Sunnah. [3]

Bequest (Waseeyah): In pre-Islamic Arab culture, the property of the

---

[1] Soorah an-Nisaa (4):29.

[2] Soorah al-A'raaf (7):158.

[3] al-Madkhal, p. 89-90.

deceased was inherited by his children, and parents would only inherit if a bequest were made. [1] Thus, in the early stages of Islaam, Allaah made the writing of a bequest for parents and relatives compulsory, in order to teach the new community of Muslims the importance of family rights with regard to their wealth.

كُتِبَ عَلَيْكُمْ إِذَا حَضَرَ أَحَدَكُمُ ٱلْمَوْتُ إِن تَرَكَ خَيْرًا ٱلْوَصِيَّةُ
لِلْوَالِدَيْنِ وَٱلْأَقْرَبِينَ بِٱلْمَعْرُوفِ حَقًّا عَلَى ٱلْمُتَّقِينَ

"It is prescribed that when death approaches any of you, if he leaves behind any goods, that he make a bequest to parents and next of kin, according to what is reasonable. This is due from the pious." [2]

However, after the community willingly accepted this law and they began to strictly put it into practise, Allaah replaced it by revealing in the Qur'aan a clearly defined system of inheritance laws. And the Prophet (ﷺ) further confirmed the abrogation of the old laws by stating, *"Surely Allaah has given everyone with a right (to inheritance) his right, so there should be no bequest for inheritors."* [3]

Mourning Period: The widow's mourning period was originally a full year, and it was compulsory for her husband to leave in his will provision for maintenance and housing during that whole period. The Qur'aan states:

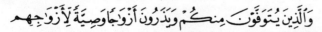

وَٱلَّذِينَ يُتَوَفَّوْنَ مِنكُمْ وَيَذَرُونَ أَزْوَاجًا وَصِيَّةً لِّأَزْوَاجِهِم

---

[1] See *Sahih Al-Bukhari* (Arabic-English), vol. 4, p. 6, no. 10.

[2] Soorah al-Baqarah (2):180.

[3] Reported by Abu Umaamah and collected by Abu Daawood (*Sunan Abu Dawud* (English Trans.), vol. 2, p. 808, no. 2864), at-Tirmidhee, an-Nasaa'ee, Ibn Maajah and Ahmad, and authenticated (*Saheeh*) by al-Albaanee in *Saheeh Sunan Abee Daawood*, vol. 2, p. 218, no. 1721.

$$\text{مَّتَٰعًا إِلَى الْحَوْلِ غَيْرَ إِخْرَاجٍ فَإِنْ خَرَجْنَ فَلَا جُنَاحَ عَلَيْكُمْ}$$

$$\text{فِى مَا فَعَلْنَ فِى أَنفُسِهِنَّ مِن مَّعْرُوفٍ وَاللَّهُ عَزِيزٌ حَكِيمٌ}$$

"If any of you die and leave widows behind, a bequest of a year's maintenance and residence should be made for their widows. But if they leave the residence, there is no blame on you for what they do with themselves, provided it is reasonable. And Allaah is exalted in power, wise." [1]

Then the waiting period was reduced to four months and ten days.

$$\text{وَالَّذِينَ يُتَوَفَّوْنَ مِنكُمْ وَيَذَرُونَ أَزْوَاجًا يَتَرَبَّصْنَ بِأَنفُسِهِنَّ أَرْبَعَةَ}$$

$$\text{أَشْهُرٍ وَعَشْرًا فَإِذَا بَلَغْنَ أَجَلَهُنَّ فَلَا جُنَاحَ عَلَيْكُمْ فِيمَا فَعَلْنَ فِى}$$

$$\text{أَنفُسِهِنَّ بِالْمَعْرُوفِ وَاللَّهُ بِمَا تَعْمَلُونَ خَبِيرٌ}$$

"If any of you die and leave widows behind, they shall wait concerning themselves four months and ten days. When they have fulfilled their term, there is no blame on you if they dispose of themselves in a just and reasonable manner. And Allaah is well acquainted with all that you do." [2]

And the bequest was cancelled by the verses on inheritance which stipulated a specific portion for widows: one quarter of all the inheritance if she did not have any children, and one eighth if she had children.

Fornication: Originally, the punishment for the crime of fornication and adultery, as well as other sex crimes like homosexuality, was the confinement and punishment of offenders in their homes until they became repentant and sought to reform themselves.

---

[1] Soorah al-Baqarah (2):240.

[2] Soorah al-Baqarah (2):234.

-22-

وَٱلَّتِى يَأْتِينَ ٱلْفَٰحِشَةَ مِن نِّسَآئِكُمْ فَٱسْتَشْهِدُوا۟ عَلَيْهِنَّ
أَرْبَعَةً مِّنكُمْ ۖ فَإِن شَهِدُوا۟ فَأَمْسِكُوهُنَّ فِى ٱلْبُيُوتِ حَتَّىٰ يَتَوَ
فَّىٰهُنَّ ٱلْمَوْتُ أَوْ يَجْعَلَ ٱللَّهُ لَهُنَّ سَبِيلًا ﴿١٥﴾ وَٱلَّذَانِ يَأْتِيَٰنِهَا
مِنكُمْ فَـَٔاذُوهُمَا ۖ فَإِن تَابَا وَأَصْلَحَا فَأَعْرِضُوا۟ عَنْهُمَآ ۗ إِنَّ
ٱللَّهَ كَانَ تَوَّابًا رَّحِيمًا ﴿١٦﴾

**"If any of your women are guilty of sex crimes, take the
evidence of four witnesses from amongst you against
them. And if they testify, confine them to houses until
death claim them, or Allaah ordain for them another way.
If two men among you are guilty of sex crimes, punish
them both; but if they repent and make amends, leave
them alone. For Allaah is Oft-returning, Most Merciful."** [1]

This law was later abrogated in the Qur'aan by the setting of a particular exemplary punishment.

ٱلزَّانِيَةُ وَٱلزَّانِى فَٱجْلِدُوا۟ كُلَّ وَٰحِدٍ مِّنْهُمَا مِا۟ئَةَ جَلْدَةٍ ۖ وَلَا تَأْخُذْكُم بِهِمَا رَأْفَةٌ فِى دِينِ
ٱللَّهِ إِن كُنتُمْ تُؤْمِنُونَ بِٱللَّهِ وَٱلْيَوْمِ ٱلْءَاخِرِ ۖ وَلْيَشْهَدْ عَذَابَهُمَا طَآئِفَةٌ مِّنَ
ٱلْمُؤْمِنِينَ

**"Flog the woman and man guilty of fornication one hun-
dren lashes. And, if you believe in Allaah and the Last
Day, do not let compassion move you in their case for it is
a matter decided by Allaah. And let a group of the believers witness the punishment."** [2]

---

[1] Soorah an-Nisaa (4): 15 & 16.

[2] Soorah an-Noor (24):2.

Furthermore, the Prophet (ﷺ) applied the punishment of stoning to death for those who committed adultery[1] and set the death penalty for homosexuals without specifying the method.[2]

A review of the abrogated verses indicates that the early law may be replaced by a more severe law, as in the case of the law for fornication which changed from confinement and punishment to lashes or stoning to death; or it may be replaced by a less severe law as in the case of the mourning period for widows; or it may be replaced by a similar but more suitable law. At any rate, in all cases, the abrogated law was suitable for the time and circumstances under which it was revealed. When the situation changed, a new law was enacted in order to realize Allaah's intent in the earlier legislation. Were it not for the situation of the Muslim community earlier, the abrogating law would have been enacted from the beginning. For example, in the case of the widow who was at first required to wait in her deceased husband's house in mourning for the period of one year during which she could not get married, it was the custom of the Arabs to confine widows and prevent them from marriage for indefinite periods, lasting from a year to the remainder of their lives. And, during the period of confinement, they were obliged to wear their worst clothes.[3] If the waiting period were reduced to four months and ten days along with the permission for them to leave their houses if they wished, the early Muslims would have had great difficulty in accepting it. Consequently, a year of mourning was set along with the cancellation of the confinement and the obligation of maintenance. Shortly after they had accepted the

---

[1] Reported by 'Ubaadah ibn as-Saamit and Ibn 'Abbaas and collected by Muslim *(Sahih Muslim* (English Trans.), vol. 3, p. 911, no. 4192 and p. 912 no. 4194).

[2] Reported by Ibn 'Abbaas and collected by Abu Daawood *(Sunan Abu Dawud* (English Trans.), vol. 3, p. 1245, no. 447) and authenticated in *Saheeh Sunan Abee Daawood*, vol. 3, p. 844, no. 3745.

[3] Reported by Zaynab bint Salamah and collected by al-Bukhaaree *(Sahih Al-Bukhari* (Arabic-English), vol. 7, pp. 190-2, no. 251).

change and adjusted to it, the new law was revealed reducing the period of mourning.

Thus, abrogation contained in it consideration for human conditions and their welfare during the era of the prophethood which ended with the death of the Prophet (ﷺ), for there can be no abrogation after his time. [1]

Legislative consideration of human welfare after the era of prophethood can be found in the fact that Islamic laws were enacted for reasons, many of which were clearly mentioned.

The following verses or portions of verses from the Qur'aan are among the many cases where the purposes for the enactment of laws were explained:

يَٰٓأَيُّهَا ٱلَّذِينَ ءَامَنُواْ كُتِبَ عَلَيْكُمُ ٱلصِّيَامُ كَمَا كُتِبَ عَلَى ٱلَّذِينَ مِن قَبْلِكُمْ لَعَلَّكُمْ تَتَّقُونَ

"Oh you who believe, fasting has been prescribed for you as it was prescribed for those before you in order that you may be conscious of God."[2]

خُذْ مِنْ أَمْوَٰلِهِمْ صَدَقَةً تُطَهِّرُهُمْ وَتُزَكِّيهِم بِهَا

"Take some charity from their wealth to purify them and make them grow (spiritually)...."[3]

إِنَّمَا يُرِيدُ ٱلشَّيْطَٰنُ أَن يُوقِعَ بَيْنَكُمُ ٱلْعَدَٰوَةَ وَٱلْبَغْضَآءَ فِى ٱلْخَمْرِ وَٱلْمَيْسِرِ وَيَصُدَّكُمْ عَن ذِكْرِ ٱللَّهِ وَعَنِ ٱلصَّلَوٰةِ فَهَلْ أَنتُم مُّنتَهُونَ

---

[1] *al-Madkhal*, pp. 90-3.

[2] Soorah al-Baqarah (2):183.

[3] Soorah at-Tawbah (9):103.

"Satan's plan is to incite enmity and hatred between you, with intoxicants and gambling, and prevent you from the remembrance of Allaah and from prayer. Will you not then give it up?" [1]

The Prophet (ﷺ) often made mention of the rationale behind his legal pronouncements. For example, in the case of the abrogation of the prohibition of visiting graveyards, he was reported to have said, *"I had forbidden you from visiting the graveyards, however, permission has been given to me to visit the grave of my mother. So, visit them, for they do remind one of the next life."* [2]

The explanation of the reasons for laws indicates that the presence or absence of laws depends on the existence or non-existence of their causes. If the benefit for which the law was enacted is continuous, then the law is continuous; but if it has changed due to a change in circumstances, the law must also change; otherwise there would not be any benefit in its continued existence. On the basis of this principle, 'Umar ibn al-Khattaab cancelled the distribution of the portion of *Zakaah* assigned for the encouragement of non-Muslims to accept Islaam which the Prophet (ﷺ) used to give out. As he explained, the need for their encouragement existed during the time when Islaam was on the rise and in need of support, however, in his time the Islamic state was already firmly established.

Legislative consideration of human needs can also be found in the methodology of legislation. In the case of laws wherein human benefit will not change with time or conditions, Allaah has spelled out the details very clearly. For example, in the case of religious rites, family laws of marriage, divorce and inheritance, laws against crimes whose harm will not change with the passage of time, like murder, fornication

---

[1] Soorah al-Maa'idah (5):94.

[2] Reported by Abu Hurayrah and Buraydah and collected by Muslim *(Sahih Muslim* (English Trans.), vol. 2, pp. 463-4, no. 2130 & 2131) and at-Tirmidhee.

and adultery, theft, and slander. As for things whose benefit or harm may vary from place to place, Allaah has legislated general laws of universal benefit which may be implemented by those in authority according to human needs. Examples of this category can be found in the laws concerning business transactions and the structuring of the society. For example, Allaah said,

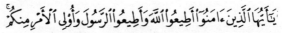

"Oh you who believe, obey Allaah and obey the Messenger, and those in authority among you."[1]

The Prophet (ﷺ) himself was reported to have said, *"If a maimed Abyssinian slave is appointed over you and he conducts your affairs according to the Book of Allaah, you should listen to him and obey (his orders)."[2]*

Legislative consideration can also be found in the giving of precedence to the general welfare over individual benefit, and to the prevention of a greater harm over a smaller one.[3] A good example of such a principle can be found in Islaam's confirmation of the almost universal practise of plural marriage (polygyny). Islaam limited the maximum number of wives to four and outlined the responsibilities of those involved. Although sharing a husband may be painful to most women, the need for plural marriage in most societies evidenced by the corruption which results from its official prohibition demand its legislation. Therefore, for the general welfare of both men and women, Islaam recognized limited polygyny thereby giving precedence to the good of society over that of the individual woman.[4]

---

[1] Soorah an-Nisaa (4):59.

[2] Reported by Yahyaa ibn al-Husayn and collected by Muslim *(Sahih Muslim* (English Trans.), vol. 3, p. 1, no. 1021).

[3] *al-Madkhal,* pp. 93-5.

[4] See *Plural Marriage in Islaam,* (Riyadh: International Islamic Publishing House, 2nd ed., 1987), pp. 1-9, for a more detailed exposition of this point.

4. The Realization of Universal Justice.

Islamic legislation considers all humans the same with regards to their obligation to submit to the divine laws and in their responsibility for breaking them. The laws mentioned in the Qur'aan are all general, making no distinction between one group or another.

إِنَّ ٱللَّهَ يَأْمُرُ بِٱلْعَدْلِ وَٱلْإِحْسَٰنِ

"Allaah has enjoined justice and righteousness.." [1]

إِنَّ ٱللَّهَ يَأْمُرُكُمْ أَن تُؤَدُّوا ٱلْأَمَٰنَٰتِ إِلَىٰٓ أَهْلِهَا وَإِذَا حَكَمْتُم بَيْنَ ٱلنَّاسِ أَن تَحْكُمُوا بِٱلْعَدْلِ

"Allaah commands you to return your trusts to whom they are due, and when you judge between one man and another, that you judge justly." [2]

يَٰٓأَيُّهَا ٱلَّذِينَ ءَامَنُوا كُونُوا قَوَّٰمِينَ لِلَّهِ شُهَدَآءَ بِٱلْقِسْطِ وَلَا يَجْرِمَنَّكُمْ شَنَـَٔانُ قَوْمٍ عَلَىٰٓ أَلَّا تَعْدِلُوا ٱعْدِلُوا هُوَ أَقْرَبُ لِلتَّقْوَىٰ وَٱتَّقُوا ٱللَّهَ إِنَّ ٱللَّهَ خَبِيرٌ بِمَا تَعْمَلُونَ

"Oh you who believe, stand out firmly for Allaah as witnesses to fair dealing. And do not let the hatred of a people cause you not to be just. Be just: for it is closer to piety, and fear Allaah for verily Allaah is well aware of whatever you do." [3]

During the era of the prophethood, a woman from the powerful tribe of Makhzoom stole some jewelry and confessed to the crime when the case was brought before the Prophet (ﷺ). Her tribesmen wanted to avoid the shame of having the Qur'anic punishment applied

---

[1] Soorah an-Nahl (16):90.

[2] Soorah an-Nisaa (4):58.

[3] Soorah al-Maa'idah (5):9.

to her, so they asked Usaamah ibn Zayd who was close to the Prophet
(ﷺ) to intercede on her behalf. When Usaamah approached the
Prophet (ﷺ), he became very angry with him and said, *"Do you
dare to intercede in one of Allaah's fixed punishment?"* He then called
the people together and delivered a sermon in which he said, *"The
people before you were destroyed because they let the nobles go when
they stole, but applied Allaah's fixed punishment on the weak when they
stole. By Allaah, if my own daughter, Faaṭimah, stole I would cut off
her hand."* [1]

Sources of Islamic Law

Islamic law during the stage of foundation was derived from revelation, either in the form of the Qur'aan or the Sunnah. The term Sunnah refers to the statements and actions of Prophet Muḥammad
(ﷺ), as well as the statements and actions of others done in his presence which did not meet his disapproval. The Sunnah is considered
the second source of revelation based on Allaah's statement in the
Qur'aan,

**"He does not speak from his desires. Verily it is inspira-
tion which has been revealed."** [2]

The Prophet (ﷺ)was given the job of conveying the final message of God to mankind.

يَـٰٓأَيُّهَا ٱلرَّسُولُ بَلِّغْ مَآ أُنزِلَ إِلَيْكَ مِن رَّبِّكَ

**"Oh messenger, convey what has been revealed to you
from your Lord."** [3]

---

[1] Reported by 'Aa'eshah and collected by al-Bukhaaree, Muslim *(Sahih Muslim* (English Trans.), vol. 3, pp. 909-10, no. 4187) and Abu Daawood *(Sunan
Abu Dawud* (English Trans.), vol. 3, p. 1218, no. 4360).

[2] Soorah an-Najm (53):3 & 4.

[3] Soorah al-Maa'idah (5):67.

And he was also given the responsibility of clarifying for mankind God's intent in the message.

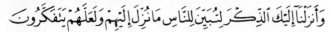

"We have revealed the Reminder (Qur'aan) to you, in order that you explain to mankind what was revealed to them, that perhaps they may reflect." [1]

Sometimes the Prophet (ﷺ) would explain the intent of the Qur'anic texts by making a statement, at other times he would do so by an act, and yet other times he would do so by both. For example, the Qur'aan commanded the believers to establish regular *Salaah* (formal prayer) without describing how *Salaah* should be performed, so the Prophet (ﷺ) prayed among his followers then told them, *"Pray as you have seen me pray."* [2] On another occasion, while he was praying a man came and greeted him, so he raised his right hand in response. [3] His wife 'Aa'eshah reported that when he made *Sujood* (prostration) in *Salaah*, he would keep his heels together. [4] On yet another occasion, he passed by Ibn Mas'oud praying with his left hand on his right, so he removed it and placed his right hand on his left. [5] He was also

---

[1] Soorah an-Nahl (16):44.

[2] Collected by al-Bukhaaree *(Sahih Al-Bukhari* (Arabic-English), vol. 1, p. 345, no. 604).

[3] Collected by Abu Daawood *(Sunan Abu Dawud* (English Trans.), vol. 1, p. 236, no. 927) and authenticated in *Saheeh Sunan Abee Daawood*, vol. 1, p. 174, no. 820.

[4] Collected by al-Bayhaqee, al-Haakim and Ibn Khuzaymah and authentyicated by Mustafa al-A'dHamee in *Saheeh Ibn Khuzaymah* (Beirut: al-Maktab al-Islaamee, 1st ed., 1978), vol. 1, p. 328, no. 654, and by al-Albaanee in *Sifah Salaah an-Nabee*, (Beirut: al-Maktab al-Islaamee, 14th ed., 1987), p. 109.

[5] Collected by Abu Daawood *(Sunan Abu Dawud* (English Trans.), vol. 1, p. 194, no. 754) and authenticated in *Saheeh Sunan Abee Daawood*, vol. 1, p. 144, no. 686.

reported to have said, "*If any of you makes **Sujood**, he should not kneel as the camel does. Let him place his hands (on the ground) before his knees.*" [1]

Thus, the Sunnah was an exposition of the Qur'aan by which its generalities were clarified and its intended meanings specified. Consequently, everything in the Sunnah is addressed in the Qur'aan, either by inference or by direct reference. The address may be so general as to include the whole Sunnah as in the case of the verse:

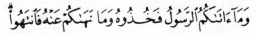

"Whatever the messenger gives you, take it; and whatever he forbids you, leave it." [2]

Or the address may indicate generally defined laws, the details of which are left to the Sunnah. Hence, the Sunnah may explain the methodology, reasons, requirements and location, or it may explain the inclusions which could not be logically deduced. An example of such inclusions may be found in the case of forbidden foods beyond those mentioned in the Qur'aan. Allaah does state in reference to the Prophet (ﷺ):

وَيُحِلُّ لَهُمُ ٱلطَّيِّبَٰتِ وَيُحَرِّمُ عَلَيْهِمُ ٱلْخَبَٰئِثَ

"He made lawful for them the good (and pure) things and forbade them the bad (and impure)." [3]

Anas ibn Maalik said, "*On the day of the Battle of Khaybar, a visitor came and said, 'Oh messenger of Allaah, the donkeys have been eaten.' Then another came and said, 'Oh messenger of Allaah, the donkeys are being destroyed.' Allaah's messenger (ﷺ) then sent Abu Talhah to*

---

[1] Collected by Abu Daawood *(Sunan Abu Dawud* (English Trans.), vol. 1, p. 215, no. 839) and authenticated in *Saheeh Sunan Abee Daawood*, vol. 1, p. 158, no. 746.

[2] Soorah al-Hashr (59):7.

[3] Soorah al-A'raaf (7):157.

make an announcement: Allaah and His Messenger have prohibited you from eating the flesh of domesticated donkeys, for it is bad (and impure)." [1]

Or the address may indicate general principles from which the Prophet (ﷺ) may deduce rulings. Such rulings may be confirmed by Allaah if correct, or corrected by Allaah if incorrect. Among what appears to be confirmed deduced rulings is the case of marriage to a woman and her maternal or paternal aunt. The Qur'aan forbids marrying a woman and her daughter or the simultaneous marriage of two sisters, then says,

وَأُحِلَّ لَكُم مَّا وَرَآءَ ذَٰلِكُمْ

"Except for these, all others are lawful..." [2]

However, Abu Hurayrah reported that Allaah's Messenger (ﷺ) said, *"One should not combine a woman and her father's sister in marriage, or a woman and her mother's sister."* [3] This ruling may have been deduced because the reason for prohibiting the combination of a woman and her daughter or two sisters, is present in the combination of a woman and her aunt. For, among the narrations of this statement of the Prophet (ﷺ) is the explanatory addition, *"If you do that, you will break family ties."* That is, in the same way that the sanctity of the relationship between sisters, or a mother and her daughter, would be destroyed by the spirit of rivalry found between co-wives, it would also be destroyed between a woman and her aunt.

Among the examples of deduced rulings which were not confirmed is that of the *DHihaar* divorce. Khawlah bint Tha'labah said, *"My hus-*

---

[1] Collected by Muslim *(Sahih Muslim* (English Trans.), vol. 3, p. 1072, no. 4778).

[2] Soorah an-Nisaa (4):24.

[3] Collected by al-Bukhaaree *(Sahih Al-Bukhari* (Arabic-English), vol. 7, p. p. 34, no. 45), Muslim *(Sahih Muslim* (English Trans.), vol. 2, pp. 79-10, no. 3268) and Abu Daawood *(Sunan Abu Dawud,* (English Trans.), vol. 2, p. 551, no. 2061).

band, *Aws ibn as-Saamit, pronounced the words: You are to me like my mother's back. So I came to Allaah's messenger to complain against my husband. However, the messenger of Allaah disagreed with me and said, 'Fear Allaah. He is your cousin.' I continued complaining until the verse was revealed:*

قَدْ سَمِعَ ٱللَّهُ قَوْلَ ٱلَّتِي تُجَـٰدِلُكَ فِى زَوْجِهَا وَتَشْتَكِىٓ إِلَى ٱللَّهِ وَٱللَّهُ يَسْمَعُ تَحَاوُرَكُمَآ إِنَّ ٱللَّهَ سَمِيعٌۢ بَصِيرٌ ۞ ٱلَّذِينَ يُظَٰهِرُونَ مِنكُم مِّن نِّسَآئِهِم مَّا هُنَّ أُمَّهَٰتِهِمْ إِنْ أُمَّهَٰتُهُمْ إِلَّا ٱلَّٰٓـِٔى وَلَدْنَهُمْ وَإِنَّهُمْ لَيَقُولُونَ مُنكَرًا مِّنَ ٱلْقَوْلِ وَزُورًا

"Allaah has indeed heard the statement of the woman who disputed with you concerning her husband and carried her complaint to Allaah, and Allaah hears your discussion. Surely Allaah hears and sees all things. If any men among you declare their wives like their mothers (DHihaar), they cannot be their mothers. None can be their mothers except those who gave birth to them. They use bad words and falsehood..."[1] [2]

The Prophet (ﷺ) had accepted *DHihaar* as being a valid form of divorce and had told Khawlah to accept it, however Allaah declared it invalid.

There also exists another category of unconfirmed deduced rulings which demonstrate that the Sunnah is limited to confirmed religious rulings and exclude personal habits and customs of the Prophet (ﷺ)

---

[1] Soorah al-Mujaadalah (58):1-3.

[2] Collected by Abu Daawood (*Sunan Abu Dawud* (English Trans.), vol. 2, p. 598, no. 2208) and authenticated in *Saheeh Sunan Abee Daawood*, vol. 2, pp. 417-8.

which he did not instruct his followers to follow. Raafi' ibn Khadeej reported that Allaah's Messenger (ﷺ) came to Madeenah and found the people grafting their date-palm trees. He asked them what they were doing and they informed him that they were artifically pollinating the trees. He then said, *"Perhaps it would be better if you did not do that."* When they abandoned the practise, the yield of the date-palms became less. So they informed him and he said, *"I am a human being. So when I tell you to do something pertaining to the religion, accept it, but when I tell you something from my personal opinion, keep in mind that I am a human being."* Anas reported that he added, *"You have better knowledge (of technical skills) in the affairs of this world."* [1]

The Prophet (ﷺ) further informed his followers that even in the case of legal judgements with regard to disputes brought before him, he could unintentionally rule incorrectly, as some of such decisions were based on his own opinion. Umm Salamah reported that Allaah's Messenger (ﷺ) said, *"I am only a human being, and you bring your disputes to me. Perhaps some of you are more eloquent in their plea than others, and I judge in their favor according to what I hear from them. So, whatever I rule in anyone's favor which belongs to his brother, he should not take any of it, because I have only granted him a piece of Hell."* [2] Such decisions based on personal reasoning represented training for the companions of the Prophet (ﷺ) in the methodology of application of the Sharee'ah. It taught them that a judge is not held responsible if he makes a mistake in judgement due to factors beyond his control. And, in order to further emphasize this important point, the Prophet (ﷺ) also said, *"Whoever makes a reasoned decision (Ijtihaad) and is correct will receive two rewards,*

---

[1] Reported by Raafi' ibn Khadeej and Anas, and collected by Muslim *(Sahih Muslim* (English Trans.), vol. 4, p. 1259, no. 5831 & 5832).

[2] Collected by Abu Daawood *(Sunan Abu Dawud* (English Trans.), vol. 3, p. 1016, no. 3576) and authenticated in *Saheeh Sunan Abee Daawood*, vol. 2, p. 684, no. 3058.

while he who does so and is incorrect will receive one reward." [1] However, such decisions have to be based on knowledge, for the messenger of Allaah (ﷺ) also said, "*There are three types of judges; one who will go to paradise and two who will go to Hell. The one in paradise is the man who knows the truth and judges according to it. The man who knows the truth and is unjust in his judgement will be in Hell. And the man without knowledge who makes judgement for people will also go to Hell.*" [2] The Prophet (ﷺ) also encouraged his companions to make legal rulings in order to prepare them to carry on the application of the *Sharee'ah* after he left them.

'Alee ibn Abee Ṭaalib said, "*Allaah's messenger (ﷺ) sent me to Yemen as a judge, so I asked, 'Oh messenger of Allaah! You are sending me and I am young, and I have no knowledge of giving judgement?' He replied, 'Allaah will guide your heart and keep your tongue firmly (attached to the truth). When two litigants sit before you, do not decide until you have heard what the other has to say the way you heard the first, for it is more suitable for the correct judgement to become clear to you.'* " [3]

Abu Sa'eed al-Khudree was reported to have said, "*The QuraydHah tribe surrendered on the condition that it would be Sa'd ibn Mu'aadh who would pass judgement on them, so the Messenger of Allaah (ﷺ) sent for him. When Sa'd approached the Masjid riding on a donkey, Allaah's messenger (ﷺ) said to the Ansaar (Muslims of Madeenah), 'Stand up to receive you chief.' And he said to Sa'd,*

---

[1] Reported by 'Amr ibn al-'Aaṣ and collected by al-Bukhaaree *(Sahih Al-Bukhari* (Arabic-English), vol. 9, p. 330, no. 450) and Abu Daawood *(Sunan Abu Dawud* (English Trans.), vol. 3, pp. 1013-4, no. 3567).

[2] Reported by Buraydah and collected by Abu Daawood *(Sunan Abu Dawud* (English Trans.), vol. 3, p. 1013, no. 3566) and authenticated in *Saheeh Sunan Abee Daawood*, vol. 2, p. 682, no. 3051.

[3] Collected by Abu Daawood *(Sunan Abu Dawud* (English Trans.), vol. 3, p. 1016, no. 3576) and authenticated in *Saheeh Sunan Abee Daawood*, vol. 2, p. 684, no. 3057.

'These people have surrendered accepting your decision.' Sa'd said, 'Execute their warriors and take their women and children as prisoners.' On hearing that the Prophet (ﷺ) said, 'You have judged according to Allaah's judgement.' " [1]

The process of arriving at reasoned decisions to suit new circumstances and the decisions themselves are referred to as *Ijtihaad*. As has been seen, both the Prophet (ﷺ) and his companions practised *Ijtihaad* during this stage in the development of Islamic law. However, it should be noted that the *Ijtihaads* of the Prophet (ﷺ) which occured during this period are not considered an independant source of law, because their validity depended on divine revelation for confirmation. Thus, the *Ijtihaads* of the Prophet (ﷺ) were essentially a means of giving the companions lessons in the methods of *Ijtihaad,* and the *Ijtihaads* of the *Sahaabah,* at this early stage, were basically for practice.

Section Summary

1. Islamic law in this early period consisted of the laws of *Sharee'ah* which were revealed and recorded in the Qur'aan and the Sunnah. They relate mainly to the ideological foundation of Islaam, *Eemaan,* and the socio-economic laws necessary for the organization of the fledgling Muslim state.

2. The basis of legislation in the Qur'aan was that of human reformation, as such, beneficial human customs and practises were recognized and incorporated into the body of divine legislation.

3. In order to achieve the goal of reformation, Qur'anic legislation incorporated the principles of:

   a) Removal of difficulty

   b) Reduction of religious obligations

---

[1] Collected by Muslim *(Sahih Muslim* (English Trans.), vol. 3, p. 966, no. 4368).

c) Realization of public welfare

d) Realization of universal justice.

4. This period marked the beginning of the evolution of *Fiqh* and it was during this period that the foundations for the science of deducing laws from the Qur'aan and the Sunnah were laid by the Prophet (ﷺ).

5. It might be said that in this period the first *Madh-hab* (school of legal thought) took shape as the Prophet (ﷺ) guided and trained the *Sahaabah* in *Ijtihaad*.

2 THE SECOND STAGE: ESTABLISHMENT

This stage represents the era of the Righteous Caliphs[1] and the major *Sahaabah* (companions of the Prophet (ﷺ). It extends from the caliphate of Abu Bakr (632-634CE) to the death of the fourth Caliph 'Alee (661CE). The borders of the Islamic state were rapidly expanded during the first twenty years of this stage to include Syria, Jordan, Egypt, Iraq, and Persia. Thus, Muslims were suddenly brought into contact with totally new systems, cultures, and patterns of behaviour for which specific provision was not to be found in the laws of *Sharee'ah*. To deal with the numerous new problems, the Righteous Caliphs relied heavily on decisions by consensus *(Ijmaa')* as well as *Ijtihaad*, in which they had been trained by the Prophet (ﷺ) while they were with him after his migration to Madeenah. In the course of their extensive use of *Ijmaa'* and *Ijtihaad*, these caliphs established procedures which later became the basis for legislation in Islaam, that is *Fiqh*.

In this section we shall examine, in some detail, the problem-solving procedures developed by the Righteous Caliphs and the general approach used by individual *Sahaabah* in making deductions. We shall also attempt to show why this period was comparatively free of that factionalism which marked later periods, and we shall note certain characteristics of *Fiqh* during this period, some of which are in strong contrast with later developments.

Problem-solving Procedures of the Righteous Caliphs

Faced with a new problem, the caliph of this period would generally take the following steps in order to solve it:
(1) He would first search for a specific ruling on the problem in the Qur'aan.

---

[1] The Righteous Caliphs Abu Bakr, 'Umar, 'Uthmaan and 'Alee, were four of the closest companions of the Prophet (ﷺ), who presided over the Muslim state after the Prophet's (ﷺ) death.

(2) If he did not find the answer there, he would then search for a ruling on it in the Sunnah, the sayings and actions of Prophet (ﷺ).

(3) If he still did not find the answer, he would then call a meeting of the major *Sahaabah* and try to get unanimous agreement on a solution to the problem. (This unanimity was referred to as *Ijmaa'*.)

(4) If unanimity could not be arrived at, he would then take the position of the majority.

(5) If, however, differences were so great that no over-whelming majority opinion could be determined, the caliph would make his own *Ijtihaad*, which would then become law. It should also be noted that the caliph had the right to over-rule the consensus[1].

The Approach of Individual Sahaabah to Ijtihaad

In addition to formal meetings of the major *Sahaabah* which were called by the caliphs for decision-making, there arose many day-to-day situations where individual *Sahaabah* were asked to make rulings. In such cases they tended to follow three general courses of action.

In the first place, *Sahaabah* who were in decision-making positions made it clear that their deductions were not necessarily as Allaah intended. For example, when Ibn Mas'ood was questioned about the inheritance rights of a woman who had been married without a defined *Mahr* (dowry), he said, "I am giving my opinion about her. If it is correct, then it is from Allaah, but if it is incorrect, then it is from me and Satan."[2]

---

[1] *al-Madkhal*, pp. 107.

[2] Collected by at-Tirmidhee, an-Nasaa'ee and Abu Daawood *(Sunan Abu Dawud* (English Trans.), vol. 2, p. 567, no. 2111) and authenticated by al-Albaanee in *Saheeh Sunan Abu Daawood*, vol. 2, pp. 397-8, no. 1858.
Sa'eed reported that 'Umar used to say that the *Deyah* (compensation for accidental murder) is given to male paternal relatives of the husband and the woman does not inherit anything from the *Deyah* of her husband, until ad-Dahhaak ibn Sufyaan said to him, "Allaah's Messenger (ﷺ) wrote to me to give Ashyam ad-Dibaabee's wife from her husband's *Deyah*." So 'Umar withdrew his opinion. (Collected by Abu Daawood *(Sunan Abu Dawud*, (English =

Secondly, if they made different rulings on a problem in their individual capacities and were later informed of an authentic *(Hadeeth)* saying or action of the Prophet (ﷺ) on the subject, they would immediately accept it dropping all differences. For example, after the Prophet's (ﷺ) death, the *Sahaabah* held different opinions as to where he should be buried. When Abu Bakr related to them that he had heard the Prophet (ﷺ) say that prophets are buried in the spot where they die, they dropped their differences and dug his grave beneath his bed in his wife 'Aa'eshah's house.

Finally, when neither authentic proof nor unanimity could be arrived at, the companions of the Prophet (ﷺ) used to respect the opinions of each other and would not force other *Sahaabah* to follow any individual opinion. The only exception to this rule was if they found people following practices which though formerly acceptable later became prohibited. For example, *Mut'ah,* a pre-Islamic form of temporary marriage which had been allowed in the early stages of Islaam, was forbidden by the time of the Prophet's (ﷺ) death. Some of the *Sahaabah* were unaware of the prohibition and thus continued to practice temporary marriage during Abu Bakr's caliphate and the first half of 'Umar's caliphate. When 'Umar became aware of the practice of *Mut'ah,* he forbade it and prescribed a severe punishment for the offence.[1]

The Absence of Factionalism

Although the *Sahaabah* debated and differed on various points of law, their differences rarely reached the level of disunity and factionalism which characterized later periods. This was mainly due to

---

= Trans.), vol. 2, p. 826, no. 2921) and authenticated by al-Albaanee in *Saheeh Sunan Abu Daawood,* (Beirut: al-Maktab al-Islaamee, 1989), vol. 2, p. 565, no. 2540).

[1] Abdul Hamid Siddiqi, *Sahih Muslim,* (Lahore: SH. Muhammad Ashraf, 1976) vol. 2, pp. 610-1.

the following factors which tended to preserve their unity:

(1) The Caliphs' reliance on mutual consultation *(Shooraa)* to arrive at a ruling.

(2) The ease with which a consensus could be arrived at. It was easy to hold consultative meetings since the early caliphs did not allow the *Sahaabah* to move far from the capital of the Islamic state, Madeenah.

(3) The general reluctance of individual *Sahaabah* to make legal rulings *(Fatwaas)*. Instead, they tended to re-direct puzzling questions to other *Sahaabah* who were better qualified to answer them.

(4) The infrequent quotation of *Hadeeth*, which they tended to confine to specific and actual problems. This was due to:

(a) Their fear of misquoting the Prophet (ﷺ) who had said, *"Whoever tells a lie in my name will find his seat in the fire."*[1]

(b) The fact that Caliph 'Umar ibn al-Khattaab forbade excessive quotation of *Hadeeth* and ordered the *Sahaabah* to concentrate on the narration and study of the Qur'aan.

Characteristics of *Fiqh* During This Period

As we trace the historical development of *Fiqh* and the evolution of *Madh-habs*, we can see that *Fiqh* showed different characteristic trends during different periods of political and socio-economic development. First, we can discern that the outstanding characteristic of *Fiqh* during the period of the Righteous Caliphs was its realism; that is, it was based on actual problems rather than on hypothetical or imaginary ones. This realistic form of *Fiqh* was later referred to in Arabic as *al-Fiqh al-Waqi'ee* (realistic *Fiqh*) to distinguish it from the hypothetical *Fiqh* advocated by the "Reasoning People" *(Ahl ar-Ra'i)* who came to prominence in Kufah, Iraq, during the time of the Umayyads.

---

[1] Collected by al-Bukhaaree *(Sahih Al-Bukhari* (Arabic-English), vol. 4, p. 442, no. 667) and Abu Daawood *(Sunan Abu Dawud* (English Trans.), vol. 3, p. 1036, no. 3643).

Secondly, although the Righteous Caliphs tended, as we have noted above, to follow certain procedures to achieve legal rulings, neither they nor the *Sahaabah* as a whole prescribed set procedures to be followed throughout the Islamic nation (the *Ummah);* nor did they make a record of the laws resulting from their legal rulings. This openmindedness in areas not clearly defined by *Sharee'ah* reflects, in the first place, the *Sahaabah's* respect for freedom of opinion in such matters. Such an attitude contrasts strongly with the appearance of rigidity on the part of certain later scholars. In the second place, it was in keeping with the *Sahaabah's* policy of recommending for the masses the careful study of the Qur'aan without the distraction of legal rulings on matters not defined therein.

A third characteristic of *Fiqh* in this period relates to the use of personal opinion in making legal rulings. The majority of the *Sahaabah* preferred to stick closely to the literal meanings of texts of the Qur'aan and the Sunnah. As a general practice, they avoided giving personal interpretations. Ibn 'Umar, one of the leading jurists among the *Sahaabah* who remained in Madeenah all his life, followed this practice. On the other hand there were other *Sahaabah* who favored the wide use of personal opinion in areas undefined by either the Qur'aan or the Sunnah. However, they were careful to attribute resulting errors entirely to themselves, so as not to bring discredit to Islamic law. 'Abdullaah ibn Mas'ood (who later settled in Iraq) represented this school of thought.

The fourth characteristic of *Fiqh* in the period of the Righteous Caliphs concerns the modification of some laws of *Sharee'ah*, owing to one or another of two factors: the disappearance of the reason for the law's existence, or a change in social conditions. An example of the first is the prohibition by Caliph 'Umar of the practice of giving cash gifts from the central treasury *(Bayt al-Maal)* to newly converted Muslims and to those leaning towards the acceptance of Islaam. 'Umar reasoned that the practice had been followed by the Prophet (ﷺ) in the early stages of Islaam, when there was urgent need for all possible support, but that there was no longer any need to canvass for supporters. The second factor mentioned above (changing social conditions) prompted a change in the divorce law. Owing to the tremendous influx of wealth from newly acquired territories, marriage (both single and multiple) became easier to contract and, consequently, divorce became alarmingly more frequent. To discourage abuse of divorce, Caliph 'Umar altered an aspect of the law. In the time of the Prophet (鑾) the pronouncement of three divorce statements at any one time was considered to be merely one divorce statement and it was reversible. Caliph 'Umar declared such multiple pronouncements to be binding and therefore irreversible.

Fifthly, the *Madh-hab* during the period of the Righteous Caliphs was unified and directly linked to the state as in the time of the Prophet (鑾). The *Madh-hab* under each of the caliphs was that of the caliph himself since the caliph in each case had the final say in all legal decisions involving *Ijtihaad* or *Ijmaa'*. Consequently, deduced rulings made by a caliph were never openly opposed by his successors during his lifetime. However, when the succeeding caliph came to power, his *Madh-hab* would then be given precedence over that of his predecessor and the deduced rulings of his predecessor would be changed to conform with his opinion.

Section Summary

1. The basis of the deductive *Fiqh* principles, *Ijmaa'* and *Qiyaas (Ijtihaad)*, was laid during the time of the Righteous Caliphs.

2. The sudden addition of vast new territories brought Muslims into sudden contact with many different cultures, and this produced a host of new problems which were not specifically covered by the laws of *Sharee'ah*.

3. Legal rulings became increasingly necessary, and the Righteous Caliphs gradually developed certain procedures for arriving at *Ijtihaad* with a minimum of disagreement.

4. The *Sahaabah* in general also followed decision-making procedures which helped them to avoid hard and fast rulings.

5. The combined approval of the Righteous Caliphs and the *Sahaabah* in the matter of legal rulings tended to promote unity and to provide little or no occasion for factionalism within the Islamic nation.

6. Only one *Madh-hab* existed during the period of the Righteous Caliphs. This unified approach to *Fiqh* prevented the rise of *Madh-habs* not linked to the state until the end of the period.

7. Particular emphasis was placed on the study of the Qur'aan by the masses, while excessive quotation of *Hadeeths* was discouraged.

8. Although there was some difference of approach among the *Sahaabah* in the matter of the use of personal opinion, this difference did not in fact result in any factionalism during the period under review.

9. So far as *Fiqh* was concerned, there continued to be one general approach, that is one *Madh-hab*. However, the different practices of such *Sahaabah* as Ibn 'Umar in Madeenah and 'Abdullaah ibn Mas'ood in Kufah (Iraq) in the use of personal opinion could be seen as the early beginnings, or the foreshadowing of a division of Islamic scholars into different *Madh-habs*.

3   THE THIRD STAGE: BUILDING

This stage covers the rise and fall of the Umayyad dynasty. The Umayyads were in power for approximately one century, extending from the death of the last of the Righteous Caliphs ('Alee ibn Abee Taalib) in 661 CE and the ascendancy of the founder of the Umayyad dynasty, Caliph Mu'aawiyah ibn Abee Sufyaan, until the last of the Umayyad Caliphs around the middle of the eighth century CE.

The period was marked by great social unrest; the *Ummah* divided into various sects and factions; the Caliphate was converted into a kingship; many new practices were introduced, some of which were *Haraam;* the scholars refused to sit in the audiences of the caliphs and in fact fled to outlying areas to avoid conflict and confusion.[1]

So far as Islamic Law and the evolution of *Madh-habs* are concerned, this period is noteworthy for three main trends. In the first place, there was a notable increase in the number of *Ijtihaads* given by scholars, since *Ijmaa'* became more and more difficult following the dispersal of scholars to outlying areas of the caliphate. Secondly, the narrations of *Hadeeth* became widespread and there was an increasing tendency towards fabrication of *Hadeeth*. Finally, the period marked the first attempts at compilation of *Fiqh*, which was aimed at preserving the *Ijtihaads* of the *Sahaabah*. It was in this period too that scholars of Islamic Law first divided into fairly clear-cut schools of thought, establishing various *Madh-habs* which in later periods were reduced to four major ones.

Factors Affecting *Fiqh*

In the history of *Fiqh* and the evolution of *Madh-habs*, this period is one of extremely great significance. In view of this, the relevant political, social and religious aspects merit the fuller treatment which follows.

---

[1] *al-Madkhal*, pp. 121-122.

A. Division of the *Ummah*

Within the first quarter of a century of this period, the Muslim nation suffered a number of devastating socio-political blows which caused a number of sects and factions to appear. The most serious were those caused by rebellions of the *Khawaarij*,[1] the *Shee'ah*,[2] and 'Abdullaah ibn az-Zubayr and his followers.[3] The constant vying of these contending elements for control of the government resulted in a general state of turmoil.

The first two factions, the *Khawaarij* and the *Shee'ah,* later evolved into religious sects which developed their own particular systems of *Fiqh.* Relying on unorthodox interpretations of the Qur'aan and the Sunnah which suited their own socio-political views, they rejected the contributions of most of the *Sahaabah* and the Righteous Caliphs, declaring them to be apostates, and elevated their own leading figures to the rank of law makers.

B. Deviation of the Umayyad Caliphs

The Umayyad Caliphs introduced a number of practices which were common in the non-Islamic states of that time, such as Byzantium, Persia, and India. Many of these practices were in clear contradiction to the *Fiqh* of the earlier period. For example, the central treasury, the *Bayt al-Maal,* was turned into the personal property of the Caliphs and their families, and taxes not sanctioned by Islaam were introduced to further increase their fortunes. Music, dancing-girls, magicians and astrologers were officially introduced as forms of amusement in the court of the Caliph. Furthermore, with the forced acceptance of Yazeed as crown prince imposed by Caliph Mu'aawiyah in the year 679 CE, the office of Caliph was converted into that of hereditary kingship. Hence the state-*Fiqh* link was broken and a significant unifying factor of the *Madh-hab* was thereby lost. Due to these factors, the Islamic scholars (*'Ulamaa*) of this period avoided sitting in the audiences of the caliphs, and thus the principle of *Shooraa* (consultative govern-

---

[1,2 & 3] See the glossary for a more detailed treatment.

ment) was lost. With each successive caliph the government steadily deteriorated into a dictatorial monarchy similar to the non-Islamic governments of that day. As a result, some of the caliphs attempted to manipulate *Fiqh* in order to justify their deviations. To combat this distortion, and preserve authentic *Fiqh* for later generations, scholars began to collect and compile the *Fiqh* of the earlier period.

C. Dispersion of the 'Ulamaa

Many of the scholars of that time fled the political centers of the 'Umayyad state to avoid conflict and confusion as well as persecution from the various competing factions. This move resulted in a break-down of the principle of *Ijmaa'* (unanimous agreement on points of Islamic law). With the scholars scattered throughout the state, such unanimity on any new point of law became virtually impossible to establish. This in turn led to a significant increase in the individual *Ijtihaads* of scholars as they attempted to deal with the multiplicity of new customs and problems in their own areas. Whenever an outstanding scholar of *Fiqh* arose in an area, the students and scholars in that region would gather around him. Often, even students and scholars from other regions would join them and in that way a number of schools of Islamic law *(Madh-habs)* evolved. During this stage Abu Haneefah and Sufyaan ath-Thawree became prominent in Kufah, Maalik ibn Anas in Madeenah, al-Awzaa'ee in Beirut, and al-Layth ibn Sa'd in Egypt to mention a few.

D. Fabrication of Hadeeth

The narration of *Hadeeths* increased as the need for information grew. Since the state had unofficially stopped relying on the Sunnah of the Prophet (ﷺ), scholars in their various capacities had to go in search of individual narrations of the Sunnah handed down by the Sahaabah and their students, in order to make their legal judgements. At the same time a new phenomenon developed: false sayings and actions began to be attributed to the Prophet (ﷺ) for the first time. For a fabricator to be trusted he would have to relay some true *Hadeeths* along with his fabrications. This led to the beginning of the compilation of *Hadeeths* and the development of the science of *Hadeeth* criticism, which aided later scholars in their *Ijtihaads* (legal rulings). However, before the science of *Hadeeth* evolved, a mixture of true and false reports worked their way into the body of Islamic knowledge and was inadvertently used by some scholars in making decisions. In this way, a body of incorrect *Fiqh* evolved, which was further bolstered by *Fiqh* decisions made by scholars who had rejected certain true *Hadeeths* because they were only known to them through the *Hadeeth* fabricators of their areas.[1]

Characteristics of *Fiqh* in the Umayyad Period

Scholars and students in the Islamic empire during this period tended to divide into two major groups. One group of scholars leaned towards limiting their deductions to available texts, while the other group favored the extensive use of deductive reasoning and *Ijtihaad*.

The first group avoided making legal rulings on an issue if clearly defined texts from *Hadeeth* or the Qur'aan related to the issue were not available. Their position was based on the obvious meaning of the Qur'anic verse,

وَلَا تَقْفُ مَالَيْسَ لَكَ بِهِ عِلْمٌ

"Do not follow what you have no knowledge of."[2]

The laws whose purposes were identified by Allaah or His Prophet (ﷺ) were used in analogical deductions[3] whereas those left undefined were not. Because of this position, the scholars of this school of thought were called *Ahl al-Hadeeth* (*Hadeeth* People). The center of the *Ahl al-Hadeeth* scholars was Madeenah and the *Fiqh* of the Madeenan school was, for the most part, practical and based on real problems.

---

[1] *al-Madkhal*, pp. 121-126.

[2] Soorah al-Israa, (17): 36.

[3] Arriving at an answer by logical reasoning based on similarities.

The other group of scholars felt that all of the various laws revealed by Allaah had identifiable reasons behind them, whether these reasons were identified by Allaah and His Prophet (ﷺ) or not. In cases where reasons for a law had not been specifically defined, these scholars used their powers of reasoning to arrive at possible reasons. Then they applied that law to other circumstances which had similar causes. Their approach was based on the practice of some of the major *Sahaabah* who had deduced reasons for some of the divine laws. Due to this group's support of extensive reasoning, they became known as *Ahl ar-Ra'i* (Reasoning People). The center of the *Ahl ar-Ra'i* scholars was Kufah in Iraq. The *Fiqh* of Kufah developed along hypothetical lines. Problems were invented and variations of existing situations guessed at, then imaginary solutions were worked out and recorded. In their discussions they often used the phrase, "What if it were like this?" and thus they were also nick-named the *What-iffers."* It should be noted that these two trends were merely extensions of trends which first appeared among the *Sahaabah*.

Reasons for Differences

The different approaches of the *Ahl al-Hadeeth* and *Ahl ar-Ra'i* scholars may be traced to certain political factors combined with the differing socio-cultural backgrounds of the two areas in which their schools of thought flourished. From the time of the last Righteous Caliph, 'Alee ibn Abee Taalib, the capital of the Islamic state was shifted first to Iraq and then to Syria. Thus, the *Hijaaz*[1] was spared much of the turbulence and influx of foreign cultures and ideas which took place at the center of the state. Life in the *Hijaaz* continued to be easy-going and simple, due to its isolation. The *Hijaaz* was also the home of the Prophet (ﷺ) and the birth-place of the Islamic state. Consequently, there was an abundance of *Hadeeths* in this region as well as a wealth of legal rulings made by the first three caliphs, Abu Bakr, 'Umar, and 'Uthmaan. On the other hand, Iraq was a new and strange land for Muslims. When the capital of the Islamic state was stationed there, it became a virtual melting pot of various cultures and

---

[1] Western coast of the Arabian peninsula including Makkah and Madeenah.

gave rise to a great number of situations and events which were outside the experience of Muslim scholars of the time. Furthermore, because the number of *Sahaabah* who settled there was small, *Hadeeths* were not nearly as available there as in *Hijaaz*. Indeed, Iraq became the birth-place of fabricated *Hadeeth* as well as the breeding ground for most of the early deviant sects. Not being able to rely on the validity of quoted *Hadeeth*, the scholars of Iraq tended to rely on *Hadeeth*, to a lesser extent than did the scholars of the *Hijaaz*. The few *Hadeeths* which these Iraqi scholars considered accurate were only accepted after the fulfillment of very strict conditions. The natural result of this development was that the Iraqi school of thought and its scholars depended more on reason and logic than on the narrated Sunnah of the Prophet (ﷺ).[1]

Compilation of *Fiqh*

During the period of Four Righteous Caliphs (632-661 CE) there was no compilation of the *Fatwaas* (legal rulings) which had been made by the *Sahaabah*. The Muslim state was rapidly expanding and everything was in a state of flux. The practice of narration of *Hadeeth* had just started and the early band of Muslims who formed the core of the state had just begun the awesome task of guiding the young Muslim nation. Thus, there was neither the time nor opportunity for undertaking a compilation of the various rulings and opinions held by the *Sahaabah*. Furthermore, the *Sahaabah* themselves tended to view their efforts at *Ijtihaad* not as infallible truths binding on the entire Muslim nation, but merely as opinions applicable to their particular time and situation.

It was during the Umayyad period that the very first attempts at a compilation of legal rulings occurred. With the change of the governmental structure from caliphate to monarchy during this period rulings were increasingly being made which went against the rulings of the *Sahaabah*. Those who had studied under the *Sahaabah* in the various centers of Islamic learning realized that if a concerted effort were not made to preserve the earlier rulings, later generations of Muslims would be unable to benefit from the contributions of the *Sahaabah*.

---

[1] *al-Madkhal*, pp. 126-127.

Accordingly, early scholars of the *Hijaaz* collected the various *Fatwaas* of 'Abdullaah ibn 'Abbaas, 'Abdullaah ibn 'Umar and 'Aa'eshah bint Abee Bakr[1]. Similarly, the scholars of Iraq collected the rulings of 'Abdullaah ibn Mas'oud and those of 'Alee ibn Abee Taalib. Unfortunately, none of these early collections have survived in their original form. They are now only known by references made to them in the books of the next generation of scholars. However, a large number of the rulings contained in the original collections have been preserved by way of narration in the books of *Hadeeth*, in history books, as well as in later books of *Fiqh*.

Section Summary

1. The first attempts at compilation of *Fiqh* were made during the period of the Umayyads.

2. The scholars of *Fiqh* during this period followed two main trends in making their rulings: that of *Ahl al-Hadeeth* (the people of *Hadeeth*) and that of *Ahl ar-Ra'i* (the people of Opinion). With the dispersion of the scholars there was a marked increase in their individual *Ijtihaads*. The overall result was the evolution of a number of new *Madh-habs*.

3. Both the principle of *Ijmaa'* and that of consultative government were lost due to the scholars' avoidance of the degenerate Umayyad court.

4. In order to preserve essential Islamic principles in the face of Umayyad divergence from the Sunnah, the dispersed scholars relied on frequent narration of *Hadeeths* and compiled the legal rulings of the most prominent jurists among the *Sahaabah*.

5. Social unrest and turmoil were prevalent during this period and a number of religious sects and political factions came into being.

6. The fabrication of *Hadeeths* in support of sectarian views arose during this stage for the first time. Scholars, therefore, saw a need to compile and critically analyze the *Hadeeths*.

---

[1] The third wife of the Prophet (ﷺ).

4 THE FOURTH STAGE: THE FLOWERING

This stage extends from approximately 750 CE to 950 CE, and covers the rise of the 'Abbaasid Dynasty founded by Caliph Abul-'Abbaas (reign 750-754)[1], its consolidation and the beginning of its decline. It was during this period that *Fiqh* took shape as an independent Islamic science; Islamic scholarship was actively supported by the caliph and it flourished as discussion and debate on controversial issues became widespread; *Madh-habs* multiplied; various compilations of *Hadeeth* and *Fiqh* were made; and Arabic translations of scientific, philosophical and theological works exerted influence on Islamic thought. By the end of the period, *Fiqh* was clearly divided into two sections; fundamental principles *(Usool)* and secondary principles of scientific, philosophical and theological works *(Furoo')*; sources of Islamic law were identified and differences developed between the major *Madh-habs* separating them from each other.[2]

The Development of *Fiqh*

In the development of *Fiqh* during this period, there were two major trends relating to the evolution of the *Madh-habs*. The first occurred during the period of the Great Imaams, founders of the major *Madh-habs*, and their major students. Although these *Madh-habs* were fast becoming distinct entities, they continued the tradition of flexibility in making and accepting legal rulings which had characterised the earlier periods. The second trend covered the period following the death of the major scholars of the *Madh-habs*. It represents the beginning of that rigidity in making and accepting legal rulings which is the main characteristic of *Madh-habs*, and consequently of *Fiqh*, in succeeding generations.

Period of The Great Imaams

The development of *Fiqh* in the period of the Great Imaams (750-

---

[1] The 'Abbaasids were descendants of al-'Abbaas, the uncle of the Prophet Muhammad (ﷺ).

[2] *al-Madkhal*, p. 128.

850 CE) and their major students was affected by the following factors.

A. State Support for Scholars

The early 'Abbaasid Caliphs made a show of great respect for Islamic law and its scholars. The reason for this lay in the fact that they owed their office to their claim that they were seeking a return to a caliphate based on *Sharee'ah* and its legitimate interpretation. Consequently, the 'Abbaasid caliphs of this period all took pride in sending their children to study under the major scholars of the time, and, what is more, some of the caliphs became scholars of Islamic law in their own right; for example, Caliph Haroon ar-Rasheed (rule 786-809 CE). Furthermore, these caliphs made a practice of consulting the outstanding Islamic scholars on most matters of *Fiqh*. A classical example is that of Imaam Maalik whom Caliph al-Mansoor commissioned to compile an authoritative book of the Sunnah of the Prophet (ﷺ). On its completion, the Caliph consulted Maalik about allowing him to make it the state constitution, which would have made the *Madh-hab* of Imaam Maalik binding on all Muslims. However, the Imaam refused to have it done, since he was aware that his compilation including only those *Hadeeths* of the Prophet (ﷺ) that were available in *Hijaaz* where Imaam Maalik had taught and founded his *Madh-hab*. He felt strongly that no single *Madh-hab* should be binding on all Muslims in view of the fact that any single *Madh-hab* would exclude the many other *Hadeeths* narrated by *Sahaabah* who had travelled to other parts of the state.[1] This is a clear example of that flexibility which characterized the founders of the *Madh-habs*. The factor of state support and patronization of *Fiqh* scholars contributed largely to the flourishing of the many *Madh-habs* which had arisen in the latter part of the Umayyad period.

However, it should be noted that although scholars and judges were allowed a greater measure of freedom of opinion, they were often subjected to severe punishment if their rulings ran counter to political policy. For example, Imaam Maalik was jailed, beaten and tortured for

---

[1] Muhammad Rahimuddin, *Translation of Muwatta Imam Malik*, (New Delhi: Kitab Bhavan, first ed. 1981), preface p. v.

giving a *Fatwaa* that challenged an official policy of the 'Abbaasid Caliph. According to this policy, the people were made to swear that if they broke their oath of allegiance to the caliphs they would be automatically divorced from their wives. Imaam Maalik's *Fatwaa* ruled that divorce under compulsion was null and void.

B. Increase in Centers of Learning

Though the states of North Africa and Spain [1] had split off from the 'Abbaasid Empire, the territories of the 'Abbaasid state were expanded to include all of Persia, India and Southern Russia, and the capital was not moved to Baghdad. Consequently, the centers of learning and *Madh-habs* multiplied.

Scholars and students from the various centers of learning began journeying back and forth in search of further knowledge about the conclusions reached by their contemporaries in other parts of the Muslim state. A good example of this is the journey of Muhammad ibn al-Hasan, a prominent student of Abu Haneefah (founder of the Hanafee *Madh-hab*), from Iraq to Madeenah in order to study under Imaam Maalik, founder of the Maalikee *Madh-hab*, and to memorize his book of *Hadeeths*, **al-Muwatta'**. Likewise, Imaam ash-Shaafi'ee, founder of Shaafi'ee *Madh-hab*, journeyed first to *Hijaaz* [2] to study under Imaam Maalik, then to Iraq in order to study under Muhammad ibn al-Hasan, and finally to Egypt to study under Imaam al-Layth ibn Sa'd, founder of the Laythee *Madh-hab*. These journeys resulted firstly in the reconciliation of some of the major differences which had arisen among scholars and ultimately in the combination of some of the schools of Islamic legal thought. For example, Imaam ash-Shaafi'ee

---

[1] An Umayyad Prince, 'Abdur-Rahmaan ibn Mu'aawiyah, dramatically escaping death at the hands of the 'Abbaasids, succeeded in reaching Spain where he laid the foundations of the Umayyad Dynasty of Cordova in 756 CE.

[2] The western coast of the Arabian peninsula which includes the cities of Makkah and Madeenah.

combined the *Fiqh* of *Ḥijaaz* with that of Iraq and Egypt and formed a new school of law, the Shaafi'ee *Madh-hab*. Here again are noteworthy examples of the flexibility of the early Imaams in their approach to *Fiqh*.

C. The Spread of Debate and Discussion

Whenever scholars or their students met, they would exchange thoughts on various Islamic issues which had arisen in their particular areas. If there was a major difference of opinion about a particular solution, they would debate back and forth until a common conclusion was reached or various options were accepted. These legal debates also took place by mail, as in the case of the debate between Imaam Maalik and Imaam al-Layth about Madeenite customs.[1]

The huge increase in the number of debating sessions, whether by mail or in face to face meetings between founders and students of various *Madh-habs* resulted in the clarification of certain important issues and the weeding out of mistaken rulings or judgements among scholars of Islamic law.

In this early stage in the development of *Madh-habs* there was a marked lack of rigidity or dogmatism on the part of scholars and their students. That is, issues were objectively analysed and conclusions arrived at on the basis of the validity of the proofs presented. In fact Imaam Abu Haneefah and Imaam Shaafi'ee were on record as stating that if a *Hadeeth* was known to be accurate, then that should be considered their *Madh-hab*. A noteworthy example concerns the law relating to the drinking of *Khamr* and other intoxicants. Imaam Abu Haneefah, founder of the Hanafee *Madh-hab*, had ruled that the Islamic prohibition of *Khamr* covered only the product of fermented grape juice (the literal meaning of *Khamr*) and did not extend to intoxicants in general. According to this ruling, intoxicating drinks made from other sources were allowable so long as the consumer did not

---

[1] Imaam al-Layth opposed Imaam Maalik's inclusion of the opinion of Madeenitees as a source of Islamic legal rulings.

become drunk.[1] However, Abu Haneefah's three main students (Abu Yoosuf, Muhammad ibn al-Hasan and Zufar) later rejected the ruling of their teacher, since they encountered reliable *Hadeeths* of the Prophet (ﷺ) clearly indicating that all intoxicants were to be included in the meaning of *Khamr*.

This free exchange of ideas and willingness to change even the rulings of the founding fathers of the *Madh-habs* vividly illustrates the absence of that rigidity and sectarianism which characterized the methodology of later scholars of the *Madh-habs*.

Period of the Minor Scholars

The development of *Fiqh* during the period of the minor scholars of the *Madh-habs* (850-950 CE) that is, the second generation of students, was affected by the following factors.

A. Compilation of *Fiqh*

In order to make legal rulings and establish principles, previous scholars were obliged to spend a great deal of time and effort hunting in various parts of the Islamic State for *Hadeeths* and *Athars* (sayings and acts of the *Sahaabah* and their students). In this period, the Sunnah of the Prophet (ﷺ) was systematically collected and compiled in books of *Hadeeth*, thereby leaving scholars free to concentrate on the comprehension and application of *Hadeeth*.

Fiqh was also compiled on a wide scale and in a systematic fashion during this period. Some scholars personally compiled their own rulings, while others, such as Imaam Abu Haneefah and Imaam Ahmad ibn Hambal, dictated various problems and their solutions to their students, who subsequently compiled them. Imaam Maalik's *al-Muwatta'* is a collection of *Hadeeths* and opinions of the *Sahaabah* along with his personal rulings, and Imaam ash-Shaafi'ee's book of

---

[1] Muhammad ibn Ahmad ibn Rushd, *Bidaayah al-Mujtahid*, (Egypt: al-Maktabah at-Tijaareeyah al-Kubraa, n.d.), vol. 1, p. 405. See also as-Sayyid Saabiq, *Fiqh as-Sunnah*, (Beirut: Daar al-Kitaab al-'Arabee, 3rd. ed. 1977), vol.2, p. 378.

Fiqh entitled **al-Umm** contains his legal rulings supported by their proofs.

Types of Compilation:

1. The early books of *Fiqh* were usually a mixture of legal rulings, *Hadeeths*, opinions of the Sahaabah and of students of the Sahaabah. **Al-Muwatta'** of Imaam Maalik is a classical example of this stage.

2. Some books of *Fiqh* were written about the basic principles of *Fiqh*, *Hadeeths* being mentioned only in order to prove the correctness of the authors' deductions. **Kitaab al-Kharaaj** by Imaam Abu Yoosuf[1] and **al-Umm** by Imaam ash-Shaafi'ee are both good examples of this type of writing.

3. Other books of *Fiqh* concentrated on the application of *Fiqh* principles with but little reference to *Hadeeths*. These books were arranged in chapters according to the issues under discussion. The six books of Imaam Muhammad ibn al-Hasan[2] and **al-Mudawwanah** by Imaam Ibn al-Qaasim[3] are examples of this type of writing.

At first, the compilation of proofs for each legal ruling on various issues included the texts of *Hadeeths* along with their chains of narrators. Gradually concern for the chains of narration decreased, and scholars merely quoted the text of the appropriate *Hadeeth* along with a reference to the books of *Hadeeth* in which it could be found.

With the de-emphasizing of the importance of *Hadeeth*, either by decreased quotation of *Hadeeths*, or by neglecting to mention their sources and their levels of authenticity, the stand of the *Madh-habs* became the most important consideration. Thus, the opinions of the *Madh-habs* were gradually given precedence over one of the primary sources of Islamic law, namely the Sunnah. In these developments lay

---

[1] The main student of Imaam Abu Haneefah.

[2] One of the main students of Imaam Abu Haneefah.

[3] The main student of Imaam Maalik.

the beginnings of that rigidity which later became the hallmark of the *Madh-habs*. However, later in this period, some prominent scholars reversed this trend, somewhat, by reintroducing the practice of quoting the sources and commenting on the accuracy of the *Hadeeths*.

B Court Debates

There were also court debates during this period which were held for the interest and amusement of the caliphs and members of the royal court. Some scholars, like magicians, singers, dancers and jesters, had become a permanent fixture of the royal court.[1] They competed among themselves for the favours of the caliphs, and they invented issues solely for the purpose of debate. As a result, hypothetical *Fiqh* took on new dimensions as it evolved from sublime origins in the era of the *Sahaabah* and the early scholars, to the ridiculous product of court debates.

Court debates also spawned competitiveness and dogmatism, since the loser of a debate not only lost monetary reward from the caliph but also personal prestige Furthermore, because loss of personal prestige also entailed loss of prestige on the part of one's *Madh-hab*, the principle of defending one's *Madh-hab*, right or wrong, came to be considered a virtue. As a result, *Madh-hab* sectarianism became rampant among the court scholars.

C. Compilation of *Hadeeths*

However, there arose an opposing trend among specialists in *Hadeeth* compilation and criticism, whereby the issues of *Fiqh* were tackled without dependence on the traditional rulings of existing *Madh-habs*. In other words, they sought to maintain the flexibility of the earlier scholars by basing their positions on authentic *Hadeeths* wherever available, rather than slavishly following earlier rulings merely because they had been made by prominent scholars. Focusing on *Hadeeth* to resolve the problems of *Fiqh*, great scholars of *Hadeeth*

---

[1] Hassan Ibrahim Hassan, *Islam: A Religious, Political, Social and Economic Study*, (Iraq: University of Baghdad, 1967) pp. 356-378.

like Imaam al-Bukhaaree (810-870 CE) and Imaam Muslim (817-875 CE) went to great pains to collect from all possible sources authentic *Hadeeths* of the Prophet (🕌) and *Athars* of the *Sahaabah*. These, they arranged in chapters according to the format established by the *Fiqh* scholars. The initiator of this trend was the last of the major Imaams, Ahmad ibn Hambal, who compiled the most extensive work of *Hadeeth* called **al-Musnad.**[1] Both Imaam al-Bukhaaree and Imaam Muslim were among his students.[2]

D. The Organization of *Fiqh*

Through translations of the great books of science and philosophy from Greece, Rome, Persia, and India,[3] Islamic scholars gained insight into new systems of reasoning, deduction and inference. This new knowledge influenced their approach to *Fiqh* which they proceeded to organize into fundamentals *(Usool)* and secondary principles *(Furoo')*. In time, *Tafseer* (explanation of the Qur'aan), *Hadeeth* and *Nahw* (grammar) developed under these influences into specialized branches of learning.

The positions of major scholars of *Fiqh* were recorded and the primary sources of Islamic law were identified and classified in order of their importance.[4]

The Sources of Islamic Law

By the end of this period, the following sources of Islamic law in the order stated became widely accepted by most scholars:

---

[1] The *Hadeeths* in his work were arranged alphabetically according to the names of the narrators among the *Sahaabah*.

[2] *al-Madkhal*, p. 133.

[3] Most of the translation occurred during the first half of this period (750-830 CE) but its effect was mostly felt in the latter half of the period.

[4] *al-Madkhal*, pp. 128-134.

1. The Qur'aan

The Qur'aan was the first source of law and its passages were accepted unanimously as being authentic. However, there were some differences of opinion in interpretation of some of its passages.

2. The Sunnah

Hadeeths of the Prophet (ﷺ) were next in importance. However, various conditions were set by scholars for their acceptance and application.

3. Opinion of the *Ṣaḥaabah*

The opinion of the *Saḥaabah* either as a group or individually was considered the third most important source of law. This source was divided into two parts according to the positions taken by the *Ṣaḥaabah*.

(a) If they were united on an opinion it was referred to as *Ijmaa'*.

(b) If they had different opinions on a single issue, each opinion was referred to as a *Ra'i* (personal opinion).

4. *Qiyaas*

Ijtihaad based on evidence found either in the Qur'aan, the Sunnah or *Ijmaa'* was next in order of importance. The method of reasoning used was a form of analogical deduction called *Qiyaas*. An example of *Qiyaas* is the prohibition of marijuana based on the Prophet's statement: *"Every intoxicant is **Khamr** and every form of **Khamr** is Ḥaraam."*[1] Since marijuana has an intoxicating effect it can be classified as **Khamr** and thus *Ḥaraam* (prohibited).

---

[1] Collected by Muslim *(Sahih Muslim* (English Trans.), vol. 3, p. 1108, no. 4963) and Abu Daawood *(Sunan Abu Dawud* (English Trans.), vol. 3, p. 1043, no. 3672).

5. *Istihsaan* (Legal Preference)

This principle involves the preference of an opinion based on a circumstantial need over an opinion based on *Qiyaas*. This principle, referred to by various names, (e.g. *Istislaah*) was used by scholars of most schools of thought. An application of *Istihsaan* is seen in the treatment of a contract for the manufacture and sale of an item. According to *Qiyaas*, based on the Prophet's statement, *"Whoever sells food should not do so until he has it in his own possession"*,[1] contracts of this type are invalid, since the item is non-existent at the time of the contract. However, since such contracts have been universally accepted by people and the need for such contracts is obvious, the ruling by *Qiyaas* was dropped and the contracts were allowed, based on the principle of preference *(Istihsaan)*.

6. *'Urf* (Custom)

Local customs were accepted as a source of law in a given region as long as they did not contradict any of the principles of Islamic law; for example local marriage customs concerning dowry payment. The dowry *(Mahr)* according to Islamic law, must be agreed upon as part of the marriage contract but it has no set time to be paid. It is the custom of Egyptians as well as others that a portion of it called the *Muqaddam* must be paid before the marriage ceremony while the remainder called the *Mu'akhkhar* is only required to be paid in the case of death or divorce, according to whichever occurs first.[2]

Another example of 'Urf can be seen in rental customs. Islamic law does not require the payment of a price until the thing being sold has been delivered completely. However, it is the accepted

---

[1] Reported by Ibn 'Umar and collected by Maalik *(Muwatta Imam Malik* (English Trans.), p. 296, no. 1324).

[2] Muhammad Mustafa Shalabee, *Usool al-Fiqh al-Islaamee* (Beirut, Lebanon: Daar an-Nahdah al-'Arabeeyah, second edition, 1978) vol. 1, p. 314.

custom that rent is paid before the rented place or object has been used for the agreed time period.

Although this process of organization and classification was, for the most part, positive development; nevertheless, when coupled with the prevailing trends toward factionalism, it served to further widen the gaps between the *Madh-habs*. Thus, we find slight variations in the terminology given to the same principle becoming sources of friction and opposition. For example, the Maalikee *Madh-hab* considered the Hanafee principle of *Istiḥsaan* unacceptable yet applied the same principle under the name *Maṣaaliḥ Mursalah*. While the Shaafi'ee *Madh-hab* rejected both these terms and applied a similar principle calling it *Istiṣ-haab*.

Section Summary

1. *Fiqh* took on a definite shape as an independent Islamic science during this period.

2. The many *Madh-habs* which had appeared in the latter part of the Umayyad period flourished and the centers of learning increased throughout the 'Abbaasid state due to state patronage.

3. For the first time the *Fiqh* of the various *Madh-habs* was successfully compiled on a large and systematic scale.

4. *Fiqh* became organized and divided into two main segments: *Uṣool* (fundamental principles) and *Furoo'* (secondary principles) and the main sources of Islamic law were clearly defined and graded.

5. The Sunnah in its entirety was also collected and recorded in books of *Ḥadeeth* by the end of this stage.

6. During the first half of this period, the *Madh-habs* under the guidance of their founders continued to experience a great deal of mutual exchange of ideas. However, under the second generation of students, there was a trend toward rigidity and a breaking down of flexibility which characterised the period of the great Imaams and the scholars before them.

5 THE MADH-HABS: SCHOOLS OF ISLAMIC LEGAL THOUGHT

In the previous chapters we have seen the evolution of the *Madh-hab*[1] within the historical context of the overall development of *Fiqh*. During the era of prophethood, the foundations of *Fiqh* were laid down in the Prophet Muhammad's *Ijtihaads* (reasoned rulings) as well as those of his *Sahaabah* (followers). During that stage, divine revelation in the form of the Qur'aan and the Sunnah (the life style of the Prophet (鏃) constituted the only source of Islamic law. In other words, there was only one school of thought *(Madh-hab)*: that of the Prophet (鏃).

In the following stage, that of the Righteous Caliphs, the *Fiqh* principle of *Ijmaa'* (decisions by unanimity) evolved and *Ijtihaad* became an independent principle of *Fiqh* under the name *Qiyaas*. The *Madh-hab* during this period was, in reality, that of each of the Righteous Caliphs, since the final say in legal matters rested with them. However, all legal decisions were subject to alteration on the basis of recorded statements or practices of the Prophet (鏃): that is, *Hadeeth*. Therefore there was no room for rigidity or factionalism.

The early period of the Umayyad dynasty saw the division of *Fiqh* scholars into two main *Madh-habs* with respect to *Ijtihaad: Ahl ar-Ra'i* and *Ahl al-Hadeeth*. These two *Madh-habs* evolved into a number of new *Madh-habs* during the shift from caliphate to monarchy when the caliph/king was no longer the head of the *Madh-hab*. Since scholars and their students were dispersed throughout the Umayyad state, their personal *Ijtihaads* increased in order to solve local issues. It should be noted, however, that during both the period of the Umayyads and that of the early 'Abbaasids, students of *Fiqh* freely and frequently changed teachers and exchanged legal opinions. In effect, therefore, the flexibility of the previous periods was maintained.

---

[1] The sum total of the scholars legal rulings as well as the rulings of his students and that of all the scholars who adhered to their approach.

As will be shown in chapters seven and eight, during the latter part of the 'Abbaasid dynasty, *Fiqh* was formalized and systematized. The number of *Madh-habs* decreased and the differences between them became emphasized due to the state's preference for some *Madh-habs* over others and the rise of inter *Madh-hab* rivalry promoted by court debates. And after the destruction of the 'Abbaasid Caliphate and the decline of *Ijtihaad* culminating in its disappearance, the number of *Madh-habs* decreased to four which evolved into completely distinct and often times antagonistic entities. The differences between them became unsurmountable in the minds of their adherents and *Madh-hab* fanaticism and sectarianism was rife. Since the applicability of *Sharee'ah* to all times and places depended largely upon the principle of *Ijtihaad,* the loss of this vital principle spelled the inevitable stagnation and decline of *Fiqh.*

In the following two chapters we will examine more closely the *Madh-habs* chronologically with respect to their founders, formation and fundamental principles. Then we will have a look at the main reasons for the differences which arose between them.

THE HANAFEE *MADH-HAB*
The Founder: Imaam Abu Haneefah (703-767CE)

This *Madh-hab* is named after its founding scholar, Abu Haneefah, whose actual name was Nu'maan ibn Thaabit. He was born in the year 702 CE, Kufah, (Iraq). His father was a silk merchant of Persian origin, who accepted Islaam during the reign of the *Khulafaa Raashidoon* (Righteous Caliphs). Abu Haneefah began his earlier studies in the field of philosophy and dialectics known as *'Ilm al-Kalaam,* but after mastering its various disciplines, he left it and went into an indepth study of *Fiqh* and *Hadeeth.* He chose as his main teacher, Hammaad ibn Zayd, who was among the greatest scholars of *Hadeeth* of his time. Abu Haneefah studied under him for eighteen years. During this time he became qualified to teach, but instead remained Hammaad's student until the latter died in the year 742 CE. After Hammaad's death Abu Haneefah took up the position of teacher at the age of forty and became the most outstanding scholar in Kufah. As such, he appeared to be a valuable prize to the Umayyad caliphs of that time. They offered him the position of *Qaadee* (judge) of Kufah, but he refused the post in spite of being physically beaten for his refusal by the Ameer of Kufah, Yazeed ibn 'Umar. Similarly, during the rule of the 'Abbaasids, he also refused royal appointment, and was consequently imprisoned in Baghdad by the Caliph Abu Ja'far al-Mansoor (754-775 CE). He remained imprisoned until his death in 767 CE. Abu Haneefah was considered among the minor *Taabi'oon* (students of the *Sahaabah*), because he had met a few of the *Sahaabah* and had related some *Hadeeths* from them.[1]

Formation of the Hanafee *Madh-hab*

Imaam Abu Haneefah based his teaching method on the principle of *Shooraa* (group discussion). He would present a legal problem to his students for debate and discussion and tell them to record its solution whenever they arrived at a unified position. Because of this interactive approach to making legal rulings, we could say that the Hanafee *Madh-hab* was as much a product of Abu Haneefah's students' efforts as it was a product of his own efforts. They would also debate on hypothetical problems and work out solutions, based on the principle of preparing for a problem before its occurrence. Because of their leaning towards hypothetical *Fiqh* which often introduced an issue with the question, "What if so and so happened?", they became known as the *What-iffers* or *Ahl ar-Ra'i* (the opinion people).

Sources of Law used by the Hanafee *Madh-hab*

The early jurists of this *Madh-hab* deduced Islamic laws from the following sources, which are listed in the order of their importance:

1. The Qur'aan

They considered the Qur'aan to be the primary unquestionable source of Islamic law. In fact it was used to determine the accuracy of the other sources. Accordingly any other source that contradicted the Qur'aan was considered inaccurate.

---

[1] *al-Madkhal*, pp. 171-172.

2. The Sunnah

The Sunnah was consulted as the second most important source of Islamic law, but with some qualification as to its use. They stipulated that it was not sufficient that a *Hadeeth* be accurate *(Saheeh)*, but it had to be also widely known *(Mash-hoor)*, if it was to be used as a legal proof. This condition was laid down as a safeguard against false *Hadeeths* which were cropping up frequently in that region where only a few notable *Sahaabah* had settled ('Alee and Ibn Mas'ood).

3. *Ijmaa'* of the *Sahaabah*

Third in importance as a source of Islamic law was the unanimous opinion of the *Sahaabah* on any point of law not specified in the Qur'aan or the Sunnah. That is, *Ijmaa'* of the *Sahaabah* was given precedence over the personal opinions of Abu Haneefah and his students in their deduction of Islamic law. The Hanafee *Madh-hab* also recognized the *Ijmaa'* of Muslim scholars in any age as valid and binding on Muslims.

4. Individual opinion of the *Sahaabah*

If there were different opinions among the *Sahaabah* on a particular point of law and no *Ijmaa'* was subsequently formed, Abu Haneefah would choose the opinion which appeared most appropriate to the case in question. In establishing this as a vital principle of his *Madh-hab*, Abu Haneefah again gave more weight to the opinions of the *Sahaabah* than to his own.[1] However, he did apply his own reasoning in a limited sense by choosing one of their various opinions.

5. *Qiyaas* (Analogical deduction)

Abu Haneefah felt no obligation to accept the deductions of the students of the *Sahaabah* *(Taabi'oon)* in areas where no clear proof was available from any of the above mentioned sources. He consi-

---

[1] Muhammad Yoosuf Moosaa, *Taareekh al-Fiqh al-Islaamee*, (Cairo: Daar al-Kitaab al-Arabee, 1955), vol. 3, p. 62.

dered himself the equal of the *Taabi'oon* and would make his own *Ijtihaad* based on the principles of *Qiyaas* which he and his students established.

6. *Istihsaan* (Preference)

Istihsaan, in short, is the preference of one proof over another proof because it appears more suitable to the situation, even though the preferred proof may be technically weaker than the one it is preferred to. This may involve the preference of a *Hadeeth* which is specific over a general one, or it may even involve the preference of a more suitable law over the one deduced by *Qiyaas*.

7. *'Urf* (Local Custom)

Local customs were given legal weight in areas where there were no binding Islamic customs available. It was through the application of this principle that various customs found in the multiplicity of cultures within the Islamic world entered the legal system and became mistakenly classified as Islamic.[1]

Main Students of the Hanafee *Madh-hab*

The most famous of Abu Haneefah's students were Zufar ibn al-Hudhayl, Abu Yoosuf and Muhammad ibn al-Hasan.

Zufar ibn al-Hudhayl (732-774 CE)

Zufar was one of those who followed Abu Haneefah's example and refused to accept appointment as *Qaadee* even though many attractive offers were made to him. He preferred to teach, which he did until he died at the early age of 42 in Basrah.

Abu Yoosuf Ya'qoob ibn Ibraaheem (735-795 CE)

Abu Yoosuf was born into a poor family in Kufah. He studied *Hadeeth* extensively until he became a noteworthy *Hadeeth* scholar then studied *Fiqh* in Kufah for nine years under Imaam Ibn Abee Lailaa (died 765 CE) whose father was a famous *Sahaabee* from Madeenah. Abu Yoosuf later studied under Abu Haneefah for nine

---

[1] *al-Madkhal*, pp. 175-186.

years, and when Abu Haneefah died, he went to Madeenah and studied for a short period under Imaam Maalik.

Abu Yoosuf was appointed chief judge of the state by the 'Abbaasid Caliphs, al-Mahdee (775-785 CE), al-Haadee (785-786 CE) and Haroon ar-Rasheed (786-809 CE). In his capacity as chief judge, he used to appoint judges for the various cities and all his appointees were followers of the Hanafee *Madh-hab*. Thus, he was instrumental in the spread of this school of thought throughout the Muslim empire.[1]

Muhammad ibn al-Hasan, ash-Shaybaanee (749-805 CE)

Imaam Muhammad was born in Wasit, but grew up in Kufah. Like Abu Yoosuf, his early studies were also in *Hadeeth*. He studied briefly under Abu Haneefah until the latter's death, then continued his studies under Abu Yoosuf and later travelled to Madeenah where he studied under Imaam Maalik for three years. During this period he became one of the main narrators of Maalik's *Hadeeth* book *al-Muwatta'* Imaam Shaafi'ee was among the many scholars who later studied under Muhammad ibn al-Hasan in Baghdad.

Muhammad ibn al-Hasan also accepted appointment as *Qaadee* during the reign of Caliph Haroon ar-Rasheed, but soon gave it up because of the many compromises which it demanded, and returned to his teaching post in Baghdad.

Followers of the Hanafee *Madh-hab*

Those who now follow the Hanafee *Madh-hab* are found mostly in India, Afghanistan, Pakistan Iraq, Syria, Turkey, Guyana, Trinidad, Surinam and to some extent Egypt. When the Ottoman rulers codified Islamic law according to the Hanafee *Madh-hab* in the nineteenth century CE and made it state law, any scholar who aspired to be a judge was obliged to learn it. As a result, the *Madh-hab* spread throughout the Ottoman Islamic state during the last part of the nineteenth century.

---

[1] Waleeallaah ad-Dahlawee, *al-Insaaf fee Bayaan Asbaab al-Ikhtilaaf*, (Beirut, Lebanon: Daar an-Nafaais, 2nd ed. 1978), p. 39.

THE AWZAA'EE *MADH-HAB*

The Founder: Imaam al-Awzaa'ee (708-774 CE)

This *Madh-hab* is named after the Syrian scholar 'Abdur-Rahmaan ibn al-Awzaa'ee who was born in Ba'labek in the year 708 CE. He became known as one of the major scholars of *Hadeeth* of the eighth century CE and was opposed to the excessive use of *Qiyaas* and other forms of reasoning in cases where clear texts from the Qur'aan and or Sunnah were available. Imaam Awzaa'ee spent most of his life in Beirut, eventually dying there in the year 774 CE, but his *Madh-hab* became widespread in Syria, Jordan, Palestine and Lebanon as well as in Spain.

Reasons For The *Madh-hab's* Disappearance

His *Madh-hab* remained the main school of thought in Syria until the tenth century CE, when Abu Zar'ah Muhammad ibn 'Uthmaan of the Shaafi'ee *Madh-hab* was appointed judge of Damascus. Abu Zar'ah began the practice of giving a prize of one hundred dinars to any student who memorized the book, **Mukhtasr al-Muzanee,** (a basic book of Shaafi'ee *Fiqh*). Naturally, this practice caused the Shaafi'ee *Madh-hab* to spread rapidly in Syria and the number of Awzaa'ee's followers continued to dwindle until the eleventh century when none were to be found.[1] However, his contributions to the science of *Fiqh* were recorded and remain to this day in most of the books of comparative *Fiqh*.

THE MAALIKEE *MADH-HAB*

The Founder: Imaam Maalik (717-801 CE)

The founding scholar of this *Madh-hab*, Maalik ibn Anas ibn 'Aamir, was born in Madeenah in the year 717 CE. His grandfather, 'Aamir, was among the major *Sahaabah* of Madeenah. Maalik studied *Hadeeth* under az-Zuhree who was the greatest *Hadeeth* scholar of his.

---

[1] *al-Madkhal*, p. 205-6. See also 'Abdullaah Muhammad al-Jabooree, *Fiqh al-Imaam al-Awzaa'ee*, (Iraq: Matba'ah al-Irshaad, 1977).

time, as well as under the great *Hadeeth* narrator, Naafi', the freed slave of the *Sahaabee* 'Abdullaah ibn 'Umar. Maalik's only journeys outside of Madeenah were for Hajj, and thus he largely limited himself to the knowledge available in Madeenah. He was severely beaten in the year 764 CE by the order of the Ameer of Madeenah, because he made a legal ruling that forced divorce was invalid. This ruling opposed the 'Abbaasid rulers' practice of adding in the oath of allegiance given to them by the masses the clause that whoever broke the oath was automatically divorced. Maalik was tied and beaten until his arms became severely damaged to such a degree that he became unable to clasp them on his chest in *Salaah* and thus he began the practice of praying with his hands at his sides according to some reports.

Imaam Maalik continued to teach *Hadeeth* in Madeenah over a period of forty years and he managed to compile a book containing *Hadeeths* of the Prophet (鬱) and *Athars* of the *Sahaabah* and their successors which he named *al-Muwatta'* (the Beaten Path). He began his compilation of *Hadeeths* at the request of the 'Abbaasid caliph, Abu Ja'far al-Mansoor, (754-775 CE) who wanted a comprehensive code of law based on the Prophet's (鬱) Sunnah which could be applied uniformly throughout his realm. But, on its completion, Maalik refused to have it forced on the people pointing out that the *Sahaabah* had scattered throughout the Islamic empire and had taken with them other parts of the Sunnah which also had to be considered in any laws imposed throughout the state. Caliph Haaroon ar-Rasheed (768-809 CE) also made the same request of the Imaam, but he was also turned down. Imaam Maalik died in the city of his birth in the year 801 CE at the venerable age of 83.[1]

Formation of the Maalikee *Madh-hab*

Imaam Maalik's method of teaching was based on the narration of *Hadeeths* and the discussion of their meanings in the context of problems of that day. He would either narrate to his students *Hadeeths* and *Athars* (statements of the *Sahaabah*) on various topics of Islamic law

---

[1] *al-Madkhal*, pp. 184-187.

then discuss their implications, or he would inquire about problems which had arisen in the areas from whence his students came, then narrate appropriate *Hadeeths* or *Athars* which could be used to solve them.

After Maalik completed *al-Muwatta'*, he used to narrate it to his students as the sum total of his *Madh-hab*, but would add or subtract from it slightly, whenever new information reached him. He used to strictly avoid speculation and hypothetical *Fiqh* and thus his school and its followers were referred to as the people of *Hadeeth (Ahl al-Hadeeth)*.

Sources of Law Used by the Maalikee *Madh-hab*

Imaam Maalik deduced Islamic law from the following sources which are listed in the order of their importance.

1. The Qur'aan

Like all the other Imaams, Maalik considered the Qur'aan to be the primary source of Islamic law and utilized it without laying any preconditions for its application.

2. The Sunnah

The Sunnah was used by Imaam Maalik as the second most important source of Islamic law, but, like Abu Haneefah, he put some restrictions on its use. If a *Hadeeth* were contradicted by the customary practice of the Madeenites, he rejected it. He did not, however, insist that a *Hadeeth* be *Mash-hoor* (well-known) before it could be applied as Abu Haneefah did. Instead he used any *Hadeeth* that was narrated to him as long as none of the narrators were known liars or extremely weak memorizers.

3. *'Amal* (practices) of the Madeenites

Imaam Maalik reasoned that since many of the Madeenites were direct descendants of the *Sahaabah* and Madeenah was where the Prophet (ﷺ) spent the last ten years of his life, practices common to all Madeenites must have been allowed, if not encouraged by the Prophet (ﷺ) himself. Thus, Imaam Maalik regarded common

Madeenite practices as a form of highly authentic Sunnah narrated in deeds rather than words.[1]

4. Ijmaaʻ of the Ṣaḥaabah

Maalik like Abu Ḥaneefah considered the *Ijmaaʻ* of the *Ṣaḥaabah*, as well as that of later scholars, as the third most important source of Islamic law.

5. Individual Opinion of the Ṣaḥaabah

Imaam Maalik gave full weight to the opinions of the *Ṣaḥaabah*, whether they were conflicting or in agreement, and included them in his book of *Hadeeth*, *al-Muwaṭṭa'*. However, the consensus of the *Ṣaḥaabah* was given precedence over individual opinions of the *Ṣaḥaabah*. Where there was no consensus, their individual opinions were given precedence over his own opinion.

6. Qiyaas

Maalik used to apply his own deductive reasoning on matters not covered by the previously mentioned sources. However, he was very cautious about doing so because of the subjectivity of such forms of reasoning.

7. Customs of the Madeenites

Imaam Maalik also gave some weight to isolated practices found among a few people of Madeenah so long as they were not in contradiction to known *Hadeeths*. He reasoned that such customs, though occuring only in isolated instances, must also have been handed down from earlier generations and sanctioned by the *Ṣaḥaabah* or even the Prophet (ﷺ) himself.

8. Istiṣlaaḥ (Welfare)

The principle of *Istiḥsaan* developed by Abu Ḥaneefah was also applied by Maalik and his students except that they called it by the

---

[1] Muhammad Abu Zahrah, *Taareekh al-Madhaahib al-Islaameeyah*, (Cairo: Daar al-Fikr al-ʻArabee, n.d.) vol. 2, pp. 216, 217.

name *Istislaah* which simply means seeking that which is more suitable. It deals with things which are for human welfare but have not been specifically considered by the *Sharee'ah*. An example of *Istislaah* is found in Caliph 'Alee's ruling that a whole group of people who took part in a murder were guilty even though only one of the group had actually committed the act of murder. The legal texts of *Sharee'ah* covered only the actual murderer. Another example is the right of a Muslim leader to collect taxes from the rich other than *Zakaah* if the interest of the state demands it, whereas in *Sharee'ah* only *Zakaah* has been specified. Imaam Maalik also applied the principle of *Istislaah* to deduce laws more in keeping with needs which arose from current situations than those deduced by *Qiyaas*.

9. *'Urf* (Custom)

Like Abu Haneefah, Maalik considered the various customs and social habits of people throughout the Muslim world as possible sources of secondary laws as long as they did not contradict either the letter or the spirit of the *Sharee'ah*.[1]

According to custom in Syria, for example, the word *Daabbah* means a horse, whereas its general meaning in Arabic is a four legged animal. Hence, a contract made in Syria requiring payment in the form of a *Daabbah* would legally mean a horse whereas elsewhere in the Arab world it would have to be more clearly defined as a horse.

Main students of the Maalikee *Madh-hab*

The most notable of Maalik's students who did not later form their own *Madh-habs* were al-Qaasim and Ibn Wahb.

Abu 'Abdur-Rahmaan ibn al-Qaasim (745-813 CE)

Al-Qaasim was born in Egypt but travelled to Madeenah where he studied under his teacher and mentor for a period of more than twenty years. He wrote an extensive book on the *Fiqh* of the *Madh-hab*,

---

[1] *al-Madkhal*, pp. 187.

eclipsing even *al-Muwatta'* of Maalik himself and called it **al-Mudaw-wanah.**

Abu 'Abdillaah ibn Wahb (742-819 CE)

Ibn Wahb also travelled from Egypt to Madeenah in order to study under Imaam Maalik. He distinguished himself in the deduction of laws to such a degree that Maalik gave him the title of *al-Muftee,* which means the official expounder of Islamic law.

Ibn Wahb was offered an appointment as judge of Egypt, but turned it down in order to maintain his integrity as an independent scholar.[1]

Maalik had other famous students from other *Madh-habs.* Some of them modified their own *Madh-habs* based on what they learnt from Maalik, for example, Muhammad ash-Shaybaanee who was among the foremost students of Abu Haneefah. There were others who developed their own *Madh-habs* by combining Maalik's teachings with that of others, for example Muhammad ibn Idrees ash-Shaafi'ee who studied for many years under Imaam Maalik as well as under Abu Haneefah's student Muhammad ash-Shaybaanee.

Followers of the Maalikee *Madh-hab*

Today, the followers of this *Madh-hab* are found mostly in Upper Egypt, Sudan, North Africa (Tunisia, Algeria, and Morocco), West Africa (Mali, Nigeria, Chad, etc) and the Arabian Gulf states (Kuwait, Qatar, and Bahrain).

THE ZAYDEE *MADH-HAB*

The Founder: Imaam Zayd (700-740 CE)

This *Madh-hab* traces its origin to one of 'Alee ibn Abee Taalib's great grandsons through his son al-Husayn. Imaam Zayd's father, 'Alee Zayn al-'Aabideen, was well known for his great legal knowledge and his narration of *Hadeeths.* Born in al-Madeenah in the year 700 CE, Zayd ibn 'Alee soon became one of the foremost scholars of the

---

[1] *al-Madkhal,* pp. 187.

'Alawee family. He narrated *Hadeeths* from all of his relatives including his older brother, Muhammad al-Baaqir.[1] Zayd expanded his knowledge by travelling to the other major centers of learning in Iraq, Kufah, Basrah and Wasit, where he sat and exchanged views with his contemporaries like Abu Haneefah and Sufyaan ath-Thawree.

The Umayyad caliph, Hishaam ibn 'Abdul-Malik (reign 724-743 CE) never missed an opportunity to degrade and humiliate the 'Alawee family and Zayd ibn 'Alee was often singled out for abuse. He was not allowed to leave the city of Madeenah without the permission of its governor and his requests for permission were often turned down repeatedly. Eventually, Zayd became the first of 'Alee's descendants to try to wrest the caliphate from the Umayyads after the catastrophe at Karbalaa. He travelled secretly to Kufah where he was joined by the *Shi'ites* of Iraq, Wasit and other places, and made preparation to do battle with the Umayyads. A number of his relatives warned him against depending on the Kufans, as it was their betrayal of Imaam Husayn which led to his untimely death, but he did not heed their warnings. Before his preparations were complete, disputes arose among his new followers when they found out that he did not consider the first caliphs, Abu Bakr and 'Umar, to be apostates who stole the caliphate from his grandfather. The majority of his followers broke away from him and declared his nephew, Ja'far as-Saadiq, to be the Imaam of the time instead of Zayd. Hishaam's army took advantage of the confusion and made a surprise attack on Kufah. Only a little more than four hundred followers rallied to Imaam Zayd's side and he was killed during the fighting which ensued.[2]

Formation of the Zaydee *Madh-hab*

Imaam Zayd was a scholar concerned mainly with the narration of *Hadeeths* and recitation of the Qur'aan. He taught in circles of learning in the cities of Madeenah, Basrah, Kufah and Wasit, and thus had a large number of students. The method used by Zayd was that of nar-

---

[1] The fifth of the twelve Imaams idolized by the Shi'ite Twelver sect.

[2] *Taareekh al-Madhaahib al-Islaameeyah*, vol. 2 pp. 749-793.

rating *Hadeeths* and teaching the art of Qur'anic recitation. If legal questions were raised, he would solve them or choose an opinion of one of his contemporaries like the jurist 'Abdur-Rahmaan ibn Abee Laylaa. The rulings of the *Madh-hab* were not dictated nor recorded by Zayd himself, but by his students.

Sources of Law used by the Zaydee *Madh-hab*

The jurists of the *Madh-hab* evolved the following sources from Imaam Zayd's rulings as the basis from which they deduced Islamic laws.

1. The Qur'aan

The Qur'aan was considered the primary source of Islamic law. The existing copy of the Qur'aan was considered to be complete without any of the deletions claimed by many extremist *Shi'ite* sects.

2. The Sunnah

The sayings, actions and approvals of the Prophet (鐌) were considered the second most important source of Islamic law. The Sunnah was not restricted to narrations of the 'Alawee family or their followers, but included all reliable narrations.

3. *Aqwaal* 'Alee

Rulings and statements of 'Alee ibn Abee Taalib which were not merely his personal opinions were considered by Imaam Zayd to be a part of the Sunnah. That is, if 'Alee did not say or imply that it was his opinion, then Zayd assumed that it was from the Prophet (鐌). However, Zayd did not accept everything attributed to 'Alee and sometimes made rulings contrary to what were claimed to be 'Alee's rulings. For example, it is reported that 'Alee ruled that *Zakaah* could be collected from orphans while Zayd ruled that it could not.

4. *Ijmaa'* of the *Sahaabah*

Zayd recognized the *Ijmaa'* of the *Sahaabah* as a source of Islamic law. Hence, although he felt that his grandfather was better suited for leadership than Caliphs Abu Bakr, 'Umar, and 'Uthmaan, the unanimous acceptance of their caliphate by the Sahaabah made it, in his opinion, legally binding.

5. Qiyaas

According to the jurists of this Madh-hab, both the principles of Istihsaan and that of Istislaah involved a form of analogical deduction. Consequently, they considered them a part of what was known as Qiyaas in the other Madh-habs

6. 'Aql

Human intellect was considered as a source of Islamic law in cases where none of the previous sources was applicable. As a youth, Imaam Zayd had met and studied under Waasil ibn 'Ataa, founder of the Mu'tazilite school of thought. The Mu'tazilites were the first to propound the principle of 'Aql; whatever, the intellect considered good was good and whatever it considered bad was bad. However, according to the Mu'tazilah, 'Aql came directly after the Qur'aan and Sunnah, and thus they rejected Qiyaas, as well as the opinions of the Sahaabah,[1] whereas Imaam Zayd placed the principle of 'Aql last and recognized Qiyaas.

Main Students of the Zaydee Madh-hab

The Madh-hab was recorded by Imaam Zayd's students. However, they also included the rulings of others scholars from the 'Alawee family as well as Zayd's contemporaries.

Abu Khaalid, 'Amr ibn Khaalid al-Waasitee (d. 889 CE)

'Amr ibn Khaalid was perhaps the most famous of Imaam Zayd's students. He spent a long time with him in Madeenah and accompanied him on most of his journeys. 'Amr compiled Imaam Zayd's teaching in two major works entitled **Majmoo' al-Hadeeth** and **Majmoo' al-Fiqh.** Together they are called **al-Majmoo' al-Kabeer.** Although all of the Hadeeth narrations in **Majmoo' al-Hadeeth** are

---

[1] *Taareekh al-Madhaahib al-Islaameeyah*, vol. 2, p. 516.

from the 'Alawee family they all have corresponding narrations in the famous six books of *Hadeeth*.

Al-Haadee elaa al-Haqq, Yahyaa ibn al-Husayn (860-911 CE)

The Zaydees did not restrict themselves to the rulings of the Husaynee side of the 'Alawee family. Hence, the opinions of al-Qaasim ibn Ibraaheem al-Hasanee (787-857 CE), who became renowned for his scholarship, were also included in the rulings of the Zaydee *Madh-hab*. However, an even greater impact on the *Madh-hab* was made by al-Qaasim's grandson, al-Haadee elaa al-Haqq, who was made the Imaam of Yemen. An Islamic state was set up in Yemen according to the Zaydee *Madh-hab* which gave it a firm footing and ensured its survival till today.

Al-Hasan ibn 'Alee al-Husaynee (845-917 CE)

Al-Hasan, known as an-Naasir al-Kabeer, was a contemporary of al-Haadee. He taught the Zaydee *Madh-hab* in Dailam and Jeelan. He was a great scholar and is considered by his successors as the reviver of the *Madh-hab*.[1]

Followers of the Zaydee *Madh-hab*

Today, the followers of this *Madh-hab* are mostly found in Yemen where it is the *Madh-hab* of the majority of its inhabitants.

THE LAYTHEE *MADH-HAB*

The Founder: Imaam al-Layth (716-791 CE)

This *Madh-hab* was named after al-Layth ibn Sa'd who was born in Egypt of Persian parentage in the year 716 CE. After an extensive study of all the then known areas of Islamic learning, al-Layth became the major scholar of Egypt. He was a contemporary of both Imaam Abu Haneefah and Imaam Maalik. In fact he carried on a debate with Imaam Maalik by mail on various points of Islamic law, one of which was Maalik's inclusion of Madeenite custom as an independent source of Islamic law.

---

[1] *Taareekh al-Madhaahib al-Islaameeyah*, vol. 2, p. 525.

Reasons for the *Madh-hab's* Disappearance

Imaam al-Layth's *Madh-hab* disappeared shortly after his death in 791 CE for the following reasons:

(a) He neither compiled, dictated, nor instructed his followers to record his legal opinions and their proofs according to his interpretations of the Qur'aan, Sunnah and legal positions of the Sahaabah. Thus, very little remains of his *Madh-hab* beyond a few references in the early books of comparative *Fiqh*.

(b) The number of students under al-Layth was small and since none of them became outstanding jurists, they were not in an influential position to popularize his *Madh-hab*.

(c) Ash-Shaafi'ee, one of the most outstanding *Fiqh* scholars, settled in Egypt immediately after al-Layth's death and his *Madh-hab* quickly displaced that of al-Layth.

It is interesting to note that Imaam ash-Shaafi'ee who had studied extensively under Maalik and under al-Layth's students was reported to have observed that al-Layth was a greater jurist than Maalik, but his students neglected him.[1]

THE THAWREE *MADH-HAB*

The Founder: Imaam ath-Thawree (719-777 CE)

Imaam Sufyaan ath-Thawree was born in Kufah in the year 719 CE, and after an extensive study of *Hadeeth* and *Fiqh* became the main *Fiqh* scholar of the *Hadeeth* school in Kufah. He held similar views to those of his contemporary, Abu Haneefah, however he opposed the latter's use of *Qiyaas* and *Istihsaan*.

There occurred between Imaam Sufyaan and officials of the 'Abbaasid state a series of confrontations due to his outspoken nature and his refusal to support state policies which contradicted the *Sharee'ah*. Caliph al-Mansoor (rule 759-744 CE) sent a letter to Imaam ath-Thawree requesting him to accept the post of *Qaadee* of Kufah on condition

---

[1] *al-Madkhal*, p. 205.

that he not make any judgement or ruling in opposition to the state policy. On receipt of the letter, Sufyaan tore it up and threw it into the Tigris river in disgust, but, as a result, he was forced to give up his teaching and flee for his life. He remained in hiding until he died in the year 777 CE.

Reasons For The Madh-hab's Disappearance

The two main factors are as follows:

(a) The Imaam spent the greater part of his life in hiding and thus was unable to attract a large number of students who might subsequently spread his opinions in the circles of learning.

(b) Although he did carry out some fairly extensive compilation of Hadeeths and their interpretations, he requested in his will that his main student, 'Ammaar ibn Sayf, erase all his writings and burn whatever could not be erased. 'Ammaar dutifully destroyed his teacher's writings, but many of the Imaam's ideas were recorded by students of other Imaams, so they have survived till today but not in an organized form. [1]

THE SHAAFI'EE MADH-HAB

The Founder: Imaam Ash-Shaafi'ee (769-820 CE)

The full name of the scholar after whom this school of legal thought has been named was Muhammad ibn Idrees ash-Shaafi'ee. He was born in the town Ghazzah on the Mediterranean coast of what was then known as Shaam in the year 769 CE, but travelled to Madeenah in his youth to study Fiqh and Hadeeth under Imaam Maalik. He succeeded in memorizing the whole of Maalik's book, al-Muwaṭṭa', and recited it to him from memory, word perfect.

Ash-Shaafi'ee remained under Maalik until the latter died in 801 CE. Then he went to Yemen and taught there. He remained there until he was accused of Shi'ite leanings in the year 805 CE and brought as a prisoner before the 'Abbaasid Caliph, Haroon ar-Rasheed (rule

---

[1] al-Madkhal, pp. 206-7.

786-809 CE) in Iraq. Fortunately, he was able to prove the correctness of his beliefs and was subsequently released. Ash-Shaafi'ee remained in Iraq and studied for a while under Imaam Muhammad ibn al-Hassan, the famous student of Abu Haneefah. Later he travelled to Egypt in order to study under Imaam al-Layth, but by the time he reached there the Imaam had passed away. However, he was able to study the *Madh-hab* of al-Layth from al-Layth's students. Ash-Shaafi'ee remained in Egypt until his death in the year 820CE during the rule of the Caliph al-Mamoon (rule 813-832 CE).[1]

Formation of the Shaafi'ee *Madh-hab*

Imaam ash-Shaafi'ee combined the *Fiqh* of Hijaaz (Maalikee thought) with that of Iraq, (Hanafee thought) and created a new *Madh-hab* which he dictated to his students in the form of a book called **al-Hujjah** (The Evidence). This dictation took place in Iraq in the year 810 CE and a number of his students[2] memorised his book and narrated it to others. This book and period of his scholarship are usually referred to as *al-Madh-hab al-Qadeem* (the old school of thought) to differentiate it from the second period of his scholarship which occurred after he reached Egypt. In Egypt he absorbed the *Fiqh* of Imaam al-Layth ibn Sa'd and dictated *al-Madh-hab al-Jadeed* (the new school of thought) to his students in the form of another book which he named **al-Umm** (The Essence). Because of his exposure to a completely new set of *Hadeeths* and legal reasoning, in *al-Madh-hab al-Jadeed*, he reversed many of the legal positions which he had held while in Iraq. Imaam ash-Shafi'ee holds the distinction of being the first Imaam to systematize the fundamental principles of *Fiqh* which he recorded in his book called **ar-Risaalah**.

---

[1] *al-Madkhal,*p. 192.

[2] Among these students were Ahmed ibn Hambal, founder of the Hambalee *Madh-hab* and Abu Thawr founder of the Abu Thawr *Madh-hab.*

Sources of Law Used by the Shaafi'ee *Madh-hab*

1. The Qur'aan

Ash-Shaafi'ee did not differ from the previously mentioned Imaams, in their uncompromising stand in relation to the primacy of the Qur'aan among the sources of Islamic law. He relied on it as heavily as those before him adding only the new insights which he gained from a deep study of its meanings.

2. The Sunnah

Imaam ash-Shaafi'ee laid down only one condition for the acceptance of *Hadeeths*, namely that they be authentic *(Saheeh)*. He rejected all the other conditions set by Imaams Abu Haneefah and Maalik. He was also noted for his great contributions to the science of *Hadeeth* criticism.

3. Ijmaa'

Although ash-Shaafi'ee had serious doubts about the possibility of the *Ijmaa'* in a number of cases, he conceded that in the few cases where it was known to have occurred, it should be regarded as the third most important source of Islamic law.

4. Individual Opinions of the *Sahaabah*

Credence was given by Imaam ash-Shaafi'ee to the individual opinions of the *Sahaabah* on condition that they were not at variance with each other. If there were conflicting opinions among the *Sahaabah* on a legal point, he, like Abu Haneefah, would choose whichever opinion was the closest to the source and leave the rest.

5. *Qiyaas*

Qiyaas was, in the Imaam's opinion, a valid method for deducing further laws from the previous sources. However, he placed it last in order of importance, considering his personal opinions inferior to proofs based on the opinions of the companions.

6. *Istis-haab* (Linking)

Both the principle *Istihsaan* used by Abu Haneefah and *Istislaah* used by Maalik were rejected by ash-Shaafi'ee and considered a form of *Bid'ah* (innovation), since, in his opinion, they were based mostly on human reasoning in areas where revealed laws already existed. However, in dealing with similar issues ash-Shaafi'ee was obliged to use a principle similar to *Istihsaan* and *Istislaah* which he called *Istis-haab*.[1] *Istis-haab* literally means seeking a link, but legally it refers to the process of deducing *Fiqh* laws by linking a later set of circumstances with an earlier set. It is based on the assumption that the *Fiqh* laws applicable to certain conditions remain valid so long as it is not certain that these conditions have altered. If, for example, on account of the long absence of someone, it is doubtful whether he is alive or dead, then by *Istis-haab* all rules must remain in force which would hold if one knew for certain that he was still alive.

Main Students of Shaafi'ee *Madh-hab*

The most important of Imaam ash-Shaafi'ee's students who continued to follow his school of thought were: al-Muzanee, ar-Rabee' and Yoosuf ibn Yahyaa.

Al-Muzanee (791-876 CE)

Al-Muzanee's full name was Ismaa'eel ibn Yahyaa al-Muzanee. He was the constant companion of Imaam ash-Shaafi'ee throughout his stay in Egypt. Al-Muzanee was noted for writing a book which comprehensively gathered the *Fiqh* of ash-Shaafi'ee. Later condensed under the title *Mukhtasar al-Muzanee,* it became the most widely read *Fiqh* book of the Shaafi'ee *Madh-hab*.

Ar-Rabee' Al-Maraadee (790-873 CE)

Ar-Rabee' was noted as the main narrator of ash-Shaafi'ee's book *al-Umm.* He wrote it down during Imaam ash-Shaafi'ee's lifetime along with *ar-Risaalah* and other books.

---

al-Madkhal. pp. 195-196.

Yoosuf ibn Yahyaa al-Buwaytee

Yoosuf ibn Yahyaa succeeded ash-Shaafi'ee as the main teacher of the *Madh-hab*. He was imprisoned and tortured to death in Baghdad because he rejected the officially sanctioned Mu'tazilite philosophy on the creation of the Qur'aan.[1]

Followers of the Shaafi'ee *Madh-hab*

The majority of the followers of the Shaafi'ee *Madh-hab* are now to be found in Egypt, Southern Arabia, (Yemen, Hadramout), Sri Lanka, Indonesia, Malaysia, and East Africa (Kenya, Tanzania) and Surinam in South America.

THE HAMBALEE *MADH-HAB*

The Founder: Imaam Ahmad (778-855 CE)

The scholar to whom this *Madh-hab* is attributed is Ahmad ibn Hambal ash-Shaybaanee, who was born in Baghdad in the year 778 CE. He became one of the greatest memorizers and narrators of *Hadeeth* of his time. Concentrating on the study of *Hadeeth*, Ahmad studied *Fiqh* and *Hadeeth* science under Imaam Abu Yoosuf, the famous student of Abu Haneefah, as well as under Imaam ash-Shaafi'ee himself.

Imaam Ahmad went through a series of persecutions under the caliphs of his time due to their adoption of Mu'tazilite philosophy. He was jailed and beaten for two years by order of Caliph al-Ma'moon (rule 813-842 CE), because of his rejection of the philosophical concept that the Qur'aan was created. Later set free, he continued teaching in Baghdad until al-Waathiq became caliph (rule 842-846 CE) and renewed the persecution. Thereupon, Imaam Ahmad stopped teaching and went into hiding for five years until Caliph al-Mutawakkil (847-861 CE) took over. Caliph al-Mutawakkil ended the inquisition permanently by expelling the Mu'tazilite scholars and officially reject-

---

[1] Bozena Gajanee Strzyzewska, *Taareekh at-Tashree' al-Islaamee*, (Beirut, Lebanon: Daar al-Aafaaq al-Jadeedah, 1st ed. 1980), pp. 175, 176.

ing their philosophy. Ahmad continued to teach in Baghdad until he died in the year 855 CE.[1]

Formation of the Hambalee *Madh-hab*

Imaam Ahmad's greatest concern was the collection, narration, and interpretation of *Hadeeth*. His teaching method consisted of dictating *Hadeeths* from his vast collection known as **al-Musnad,** which contained over 30,000 *Hadeeths,* as well as the various opinions of the *Sahaabah* concerning their interpretation. He would then apply the *Hadeeths* or rulings to various existing problems. If he could not find a suitable *Hadeeth* or opinion to solve a problem, he would offer his own opinion while forbidding his students to record any of his own solutions. As a result, his *Madh-hab* was recorded, not by his students, but by their students.

Sources of Law Used by the Hambalee *Madh-hab*

1. The Qur'aan

There was no difference between the way Ahmad ibn Hambal approached Qur'aan and that of those who preceded him. In other words, the Qur'aan was given precedence over all else under all circumstances.

2. The Sunnah

Likewise, the Sunnah of the Prophet (ﷺ) occupied the number two position among the fundamental principles used by the founder of this school in the deduction of laws. His only stipulation was that it be *Marfoo',* i.e. attributed directly to the Prophet (ﷺ).

3. *Ijmaa'* of the *Sahaabah*

Imaam Ahmad recognized the consensus of opinion of the *Sahaabah,* and placed it in the third position among the fundamental principles. However, he discredited the claims of *Ijmaa'* outside the era of the *Sahaabah* as being inaccurate, due to the vast number

---

[1] *al-Madkhal,* p. 200.

of scholars and their wide diffusion throughout the Muslim empire. In his opinion *Ijmaa'* after the era of the *Sahaabah* was impossible.

4. Individual Opinions of the *Sahaabah*

If a problem arose in an area where the *Sahaabah* had expressed conflicting opinions, Ahmad, like Maalik, would give credence to all the various individual opinions. Because of that, there developed within the *Madh-hab* many instances of multiple rulings for individual issues.

5. *Hadeeth Da'eef* (Weak *Hadeeth*)

For a ruling on a case where none of the previous four principles offered a ready solution, the Imaam used to prefer to use a weak *Hadeeth* rather than applying his own deductive reasoning *(Qiyaas)*. However, this was on condition that the weakness of the *Hadeeth* was not due to the fact that one of its narrators was class- ified as a *Faasiq* (degenerate), or a *Kadh-dhaab* (liar).

6. *Qiyaas*

As a last resort, that is when no other major principle could be directly applied, Ahmad would reluctantly apply the principle of *Qiyaas* and deduce a solution based on one or more of the previous principles.[1]

Main Students of the Hambalee *Madh-hab*

Imaam Ahmad's main students were his own two sons, Saalih (died 873 CE) and 'Abdullaah (died 903 CE). Imaam Bukhaaree and Mus- lim, compilers of the most outstanding collections of *Hadeeth*, were among the great scholars of *Hadeeth* who studied under Imaam Ahmad.[2]

Followers of the Hambalee *Madh-hab*

The majority of the followers of this *Madh-hab* can now be found in

---

[1] *al-Madkhal*, pp. 202-203.

[2] *Taareekh al-Madhaahib al-Islaameeyah*, vol. 2, pp. 339-340.

Palestine and Saudi Arabia. Its survival in Saudi Arabia, after almost completely dying out elsewhere in the Muslim world, is due to the fact that the founder of the so called Wahhaabee revivalist movement, Muhammad ibn 'Abdul-Wahhaab, had studied under scholars of the Hambalee *Madh-hab*, and thus it unofficially became the *Fiqh Madh-hab* of the movement. When 'Abdul-'Azeez ibn Sa'oud captured most of the Arabian peninsula and established the Saudi dynasty, he made the Hambalee *Madh-hab* the basis of the kingdom's legal system.

THE DHAAHIREE *MADH-HAB*

The Founder: Imaam Daawood (815-883 CE)

The founder of this school of thought, Daawood ibn 'Alee, was born in Kufah in the year 815 CE. His early *Fiqh* studies were under Imaam ash-Shaafi'ee's students, but he later inclined towards the study of *Hadeeth* and joined the *Hadeeth* circle of Imaam Ahmad ibn Hambal. He continued to study under Ahmad until he was expelled from Ahmad's classes because he voiced the opinion that the Qur'aan was *Muhdath* (newly existent) and therefore created. After his expulsion, he took an independent path of reasoning based on the obvious and lit-eral meanings *(DHaahir)* of the texts of the Qur'aan and the Sunnah. Because of this approach, his *Madh-hab* was called the DHaahiree *Madh-hab* and he became known as Daawood adH-DHaahiree.[1]

The Qur'aan and the Sunnah

Like all of the other Imaams, Daawood considered the Qur'aan to be the foremost source of Islamic law followed by the Sunnah. How-ever, only literal interpretations of their texts were considered by him to be valid. That is, they were only to be applied in the particular cir-cumstances which they described.

Ijmaa' of the Sahaabah

Imaam Daawood gave credence to the *Ijmaa'* of the *Sahaabah*. He reasoned that their unanimity would only have been on points of law

---

Taareekh at-Tashree' al-Islaamee, pp. 181, 182.

revealed to the Prophet (ﷺ) and known to the Ṣaḥaabah, but not narrated as Ḥadeeths for some reason or other.

Therefore, the Ijmaa's of the Ṣaḥaabah were not considered by him as resulting from reasoning (Qiyaas).

Qiyaas

Since Imaam Daawood limited the application of the Qur'aan and the Sunnah to their literal meaning, he automatically denied the validity of rulings based on any form of reasoned opinion, including Qiyaas.[1] However, the principle of Mafhoom (understood meaning) which he applied to the Qur'aan and Sunnah in place of Qiyaas turned out to be virtually indistinguishable from Qiyaas (analogical deduction)[2]

Main Students of the DHaahiree Madh-hab

Due to the limited scope of the DHaahiree Madh-hab and the absence of outstanding scholars to pass on its principles and rulings, it did not last very long. In fact, it did not get a foothold in any area of the Muslim empire during Imaam Daawood's lifetime, nor in the century and a half which followed his death.

In later times, all scholars who denied the validity of Qiyaas were labelled as DHaahirees, even though they had not actually studied under Daawood or his students, or even read their works.

The most noted student of the DHaahiree Madh-hab was a brilliant 11th century CE Spanish scholar named 'Alee ibn Aḥmad ibn Ḥazm al-Andaloosee (died 1070 CE). Ibn Ḥazm revived this Madh-hab and defended it in the numerous outstanding works which he wrote in various fields of Islamic study; for example, Iḥkaam al-Aḥkaam in the field of Usool al-Fiqh, al-Fiṣal in theology and al-Muḥallaa in Fiqh. Due to Ibn Ḥazm's tireless efforts, the Madh-hab took hold in Islamic

---

[1] al-Madkhal, p. 206.

[2] J.H. Kramers and H.A.R. Gibb, Shorter Encyclopedia of Islam, (Cornell University Press, Ithaca, New York, 1953) p. 266.

Spain where it flourished, and from there it spread to some areas of North Africa and elsewhere. It remained prevalent in Spain until the Islamic state began to crumble there in the early 1400's. With the disappearance of the Muslim state of Andalus, the *Madh-hab* also disappeared, leaving behind only a number of scholarly writings, most of which were done by Ibn Hazm himself.[1]

THE JAREEREE *MADH-HAB*

The founder: Imaam at-Tabaree (839-923 CE)

This *Madh-hab* was founded by Muhammad ibn Jareer ibn Yazeed at-Tabaree who was born in the province of Tabaristan in the year 839 CE. He acquired a high degree of proficiency in the fields of *Hadeeth*, *Fiqh*, and history. As a travelling jurist, he studied the systems of Imam Abu Haneefah, Imaam Maalik, Imaam ash-Shafi'ee and others. For the first ten years after his return from Egypt he strictly followed the Shaafi'ee *Madh-hab*. At the end of that period he founded a school of his own, whose followers called themselves Jareerites after his father's name. But his *Madh-hab* differed less in principle than in practice from the Shaafi'ee *Madh-hab* and fell comparatively quickly into oblivion.

Ibn Jareer was most noted for his outstanding *Tafseer* of the Qur'aan which he called **Jaami' al-Bayaan,** but which became known as **Tafseer at-Tabaree.** Of equal importance and fame was his history of the world called **Taareekh ar-Rusul wal-Mulook,** commonly known as **Taareekh at-Tabaree.**[2]

Section Summary

1. The major *Madh-habs* were: the Hanafee *Madh-hab*, the Maalikee *Madh-hab*, the Shaafi'ee *Madh-hab*, the Hambalee *Madh-hab*, and the Zaydee *Madh-hab*.

---

[1] *Taareekh al-Madhaahib al-Islaameeyah*, vol. 2, pp. 375-409.

[2] *Taareekh at-Tashree' al-Islaamee*, pp. 182, 183.

These survived largely because of state support and a body of outstanding first generation students.

2. The most important of the minor *Madh-habs* were: the Awzaa'ee *Madh-hab*, the Laythee *Madh-hab*, the Thawree *Madh-hab*, the DHaahiree *Madh-hab* and the Jareeree *Madh-hab*. These went out of existence either because of political factors or because their students failed to record the rulings of the founders for posterity.

3. The principal sources of Islamic law agreed upon by all the major *Madh-habs* were: the Qur'aan, the Sunnah, *Ijmaa'* of the Sahaabah and *Qiyaas*.

4. All of the major *Madh-habs* set conditions for the acceptance of the Sunnah as a primary source of Islamic law:

   (a) The Hanafee *Madh-hab* stipulated that the *Hadeeth* be widely known *(Mash-hoor)*.

   (b) The Maalikee *Madh-hab* required that the *Hadeeth* not contradict the *Ijmaa'* of the Madeenites.

   (c) The Shaafi'ee *Madh-hab* insisted that the *Hadeeth* be authentic *(Saheeh)*.

   (d) The Hambalee *Madh-hab* only required that the *Hadeeth* be attributed to the Prophet (   ) and not fabricated. Thus, *Hadeeths* of doubtful authenticity were considered a part of the Sunnah.

5. The controversial sources of Islamic law were:

   (a) *Istihsaan* and *Ijmaa'* of scholars, held by the Hanafee *Madh-hab*.

   (b) *Istislaah*, *Ijmaa'* of the Madeenites and their customs, held by the Maalikee *Madh-hab*.

   (c) *'Urf*, held by both the Hanafee and Maalikee *Madh-habs*.

   (d) Weak *Hadeeth*, held by the Hambalee *Madh-hab*.

   (e) *Aqwaal* 'Alee (rulings and statements of the fourth righteous caliph, 'Alee), held by the Zaydee *Madh-hab*.

6. MAIN REASONS FOR CONFLICTING RULINGS

We have seen that although the Imaams of the four major *Madh-habs* were all agreed on the primacy of the four fundamental principles of Islamic law (the Qur'aan, the Sunnah, *Ijmaa'* and *Qiyaas*), certain differences have occurred and still exist among the rulings of their *Madh-habs*. These differences arose for various reasons, the chief ones being related to the following aspects: interpretation of word meanings and grammatical constructions; *Ḥadeeth* narrations (availability, authenticity, conditions for acceptance, and interpretation of textual conflict); admissibility of certain principles (*Ijmaa'*, customs of the Madeenites, *Istiḥsaan*, and opinions of the *Ṣaḥaabah*); and methods of *Qiyaas*. Mention will be made of the positions of the four existing *Madh-habs* where relevant.

1. WORD MEANINGS

The interpretational differences which occurred over the meanings of words took three basic forms:

a) Shared Literal Meanings

There are a few words which occur in both the Qur'aan and the Sunnah with more than one literal meaning; for example, the word قرء *Qur* (plural *Quroo'* or *Aqraa'*), which means menses as well as the time of purity between menses. Thus, scholars of *Fiqh* were divided into two camps concerning the interpretation of the Qur'anic verse,

$$وَٱلْمُطَلَّقَٰتُ يَتَرَبَّصْنَ بِأَنفُسِهِنَّ ثَلَٰثَةَ قُرُوٓءٍ$$

"Divorced women should wait three *Quroo'*."[1]

The particular interpretation chosen makes an important difference when considering the case of a divorced woman who has started her third menses. According to those who considered *Qur'* to be the period of purity, the divorce becomes finalized as soon as her menses have started, while according to those who

---

[1] Soorah al-Baqarah (2):228.

viewed *Qur'* as the actual menses, it is not finalized until her third menses have ended.

(i) Maalik, Ash-Shaafi'ee and Ahmad ruled that *Qur'* meant the period of purity.

(ii) Abu Haneefah, ruled that *Qur'* meant the actual menses.[1]
Note:
'Aa'eshah said, *"Umm Habeebah had irregular menses and she asked the Prophet (ﷺ) about it. He told her to stop praying during the days of her **Qur's.**"*[2] 'Aa'eshah was also reported to have said, "I told Bareerah to observe a waiting period *('Iddah)* of three menses." [3] These narrations clearly indicate that the intended meaning of *Qur'* is the menses itself.

b) Literal and Figurative Meanings

There are also some words in the Qur'aan and the Sunnah which have both literal and figurative meanings. For example, the word لَمَسَ *Lams* (touch) is literally used to indicate touching by the hand or the coming in contact of two objects, and figuratively to indicate sexual intercourse. Thus, the jurists were of three different opinions concerning the meaning of the Qur'anic verse:

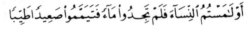

أَوْ لَـٰمَسْتُمُ ٱلنِّسَآءَ فَلَمْ تَجِـدُواْ مَآءً فَتَيَمَّمُواْ صَعِيدًا طَيِّبًا

---

[1] 'Abdullaah 'Abdul-Muhsin at-Turki, *Asbaab Ikhtilaaf al-Fuqahaa*, (Riyadh: Matba'ah as-Sa'aadah, 1st ed. 1974), p. 190.

[2] Collected by an-Nasaa'ee and Abu Daawood. See Ahmad Hasan, *Sunan Abu Dawud* (English Trans.), (Lahore: SH. Muhammad Ashraf, 1984), vol. 1, p. 71, no. 285 This *Hadeeth* is also collected by Muslim *(Sahih Muslim* (English Trans.), vol. 1, pp. 188-9, no. 652) with a variation in wording. Abu Daawood and an-Nasaa'ee's narrations are authenticated by al-Albaanee in *Irwaa al-Ghaleel* (Beirut: al-Maktab al-Islaamee, 1st ed., 1979), vol. 7, p. 199, no. 2118.

[3] Collected by Ibn Maajah and authenticated by al-Albaanee in *Irwaa al-Ghaleel*, vol. 7, p. 200, no. 2120.

"...or you touched *(Laamastum)* women and can not find water, then make *Tayammum*[1] from clean earth."[2]

This verse occurs in the context of the factors which break the state of *Wudoo.*[3]

(i) Ash-Shaafi'ee and most of his students ruled that *Lams* meant the touch of the hand or body contact. Therefore, if a man intentionally or accidentally touched a woman or vice versa, skin on skin, then both of them would lose their state of *Wudoo.*

(ii) Imaam Maalik and most of his students also ruled that *Lams* meant touching by the hand. However, he stipulated that *Wudoo* would only be broken if the touch were pleasurable, whether the touch were intended or unintended, skin on skin or otherwise. This was also the most well known position of Imaam Ahmad. They took the position that the deciding factor was the occurence of pleasure due to the existance of accurate *Hadeeths* stating that the Prophet (ﷺ) used to touch his wife 'Aa'eshah's foot in order to move it out of the way when he was making *Sujood* (prostration during prayer).[4]

(iii) Imaam Abu Haneefah ruled that *Lams* in the verse under consideration meant sexual intercourse and therefore, touching a woman did not break *Wudoo,* whether it was accompanied by a pleasurable feeling or not[5]. This posi-

---

[1] Purificationwith dust in the absence of water.

[2] Soorah an-Nisaa (4):43 and Soorah al-Maaidah (5):6.

[3] A ritual state of purity stipulated as a precondition for certain acts of worship.

[4] Collected by al-Bukhaaree *(Sahih Al-Bukhari* (Arabic-English Trans.), vol. 1, pp. 294-5, no. 498) and Abu Daawood *(Sunan Abu Dawud,* (English Trans.), vol. 1, pp. 183-4, no. 712).

[5] *Bidaayah al-Mujtahid,* vol. 1, pp. 33-34.

tion was based on the previously mentioned *Hadeeth* of 'Aa'eshah as well as another from her reported by the *Sahaabee*, 'Urwah, that the Prophet (ﷺ) kissed some of his wives then left for *Salaah* without performing *Wudoo*.[1]

c) Grammatical Meanings

There were also certain grammatical constructions in Arabic which were ambiguous: For example, the word إلَى *elaa* (to) could simply mean "up to but not including", as in the case of the Qur'anic verse,

$$ ثُمَّ أَتِمُّواْ ٱلصِّيَامَ إِلَى ٱلَّيْلِ $$

"And complete the fast up to *(elaa)* the night."[2]

The fast is continued up to Maghrib (sunset), the beginning of the night, but does not include the night itself. There is no dispute about this interpretation. However, *elaa* also means "up to and including" as in the Qur'anic verse,

$$ وَنَسُوقُ ٱلْمُجْرِمِينَ إِلَى جَهَنَّمَ وِرْدًا $$

"And We will drive the guilty up to *(elaa)* Hell like a weary herd."[3]

Thus, *Fiqh* scholars held two opinions concerning the meaning of the following Qur'anic verse describing an aspect of the performance of *Wudoo:*

---

[1] Collected by Abu Daawood *(Sunan Abu Dawud* (English Trans.), vol. 1, p. 43, no. 179), at-Tirmidhee, an-Nasaa'ee and Ibn Maajah, and authenticated by al-Albaanee in *Saheeh Sunan Abee Daawood* (Beirut: al-Maktab al-Islaamee, 1989;, vol. 1, p. 36, no. 165, as well as by Ahmad Shaakir in *Jaami' as-Saheeh,* (Beirut: Daar al-Kutub al-'Ilmeeyah, 1987), vol. 1, pp. 133-134.

[2] *Soorah al-Baqarah* (2):187.

[3] Soorah Maryam (19):86.

فَٱغْسِلُوا۟ وُجُوهَكُمْ وَأَيْدِيَكُمْ إِلَى ٱلْمَرَافِقِ

"...then wash your faces and your hands up to (elaa) your elbows."[1]

(i) Abu Haneefah's student Zufar, Ibn Daawood adh-DHaahiree[2] and some of Maalik's students interpreted this verse to mean "up to but not including the elbows."[3]

(ii) The four Imaams all ruled that the verse meant "up to and including the elbows."[4] This position is supported by the description found in authentic *Hadeeths* of the Prophet's (ﷺ) method of performing *Wudoo*.[5]

2. NARRATIONS OF *HADEETHS*

The causes of legal differences which developed among jurists over the narration and application of *Hadeeths* may be subdivided as follows:

---

[1] *Soorah al-Maa'idah* (5):6.

[2] Abu Bakr Muhammad (869-910 CE), the son of Imaam Daawood adH-DHaahiree.

[3] Muhammad ibn 'Alee ash-Shawkaanee, *Nayl al-Awtar*, (Egypt: al-Halabee Press, last ed., n.d.), vol. 1, p. 168. See also Ibn Qudaamah's, *al-Mughnee*, (Cairo: Maktabah al-Qaahirah, 1968), vol. 1, p. 90.

[4] *al-Insaaf fee Bayaan Asbaab al-Ikhtilaaf*, pp. 42, 43.

[5] Nu'aym ibn 'Abdillah al-Mujmir said, "*I saw Abu Hurayrah performing ablution. He washed his face completely, then he washed his right arm including a portion of his upper arm...then he said: This is how I saw Allaah's Messenger (ﷺ) make* **Wudoo**" (Collected by Muslim (*Sahih Muslim* (English Trans.), vol. 1, p. 156, no. 477).

a) Availability of *Hadeeths*

There were numerous cases where certain narrations of *Hadeeths*, did not reach some of the scholars, due to the fact that the *Sahaabah* who narrated them had settled in various regions throughout the Islamic empire, and the major *Madh-habs* were founded in different parts of the empire before the comprehensive compilations of *Hadeeths* were made. To be more specific, the *Madh-hab* of Abu Haneefah (702-767 CE), Maalik (717-855 CE), Ash-Shaafi'ee and Ahmad (778-855 CE) were founded between the middle of the eighth century CE and the early part of the ninth, whereas the most authentic and comprehensive compilations of *Hadeeth* (the Sound Six[1]) were not available until the latter part of the ninth century and the early decades of the tenth.

(i) Abu Haneefah ruled that *Istisqaa* (Prayer for rain) did not include formal congregational prayer *(Salaah)*. His position was based on the narration of Anas ibn Maalik in which the Prophet (ﷺ), on an occasion, made a spontaneous *Du'aa* (supplication) for rain without making *Salaah*.[2]

(ii) However, his students Abu Yousuf and Muhammad and the other Imaams all agreed that *Salaah* for *Istisqaa* was correct.[3] Their position was based on the narration of 'Abbaad ibn Tameem and others in which the Prophet (ﷺ) was reported to have gone out to the prayer area, made *Du'aa* for rain facing the *Qiblah* (direction of Makkah),

---

[1] The *Hadeeth* books of Bukhaaree, Muslim, Abu Daawood, at-Tirmidhee, an-Nasaaee and Ibn Maajah.

[2] Collected by Muslim *(Sahih Muslim* (English Trans.), vol. 1, pp. 423-4, no. 1956).

[3] *al-Mughnee*, vol. 2, p. 320. See also *Bidaayah al-Mujtahid*, vol. 1, p. 182.

reversed his cloak and led the people in two units of
Salaah.[1]

b) Weak Narrations of Hadeeths

There were cases where some jurists based their rulings on
Hadeeths which were in fact Da'eef (weak and unreliable),
because they were unaware of the unreliability of those
Hadeeths or because they took the position that a weak Hadeeth
was to be preferred to their Qiyaas (analogical deduction)[2]. For
example,

(i) Imaam Abu Haneefah, his companions and Imaam Ahmad
    ibn Hambal all held that the state of Wudoo is broken by
    vomiting basing their ruling on a Hadeeth attributed to
    'Aa'eshah in which she reportedly claimed that the Prophet
    (ﷺ) had said, *"Whoever is afflicted by **Qay, Ru'aaf** or
    Qals (different forms of vomiting) should leave (the **Salaah**),
    make **Wudoo**, then continue where he left off without speak-
    ing during it."*[3]

(ii) Imaam ash-Shaafi'ee and Imaam Maalik ruled for two
     reasons that Qay' (vomit) did not break Wudoo: First, the
     above mentioned Hadeeth was not authentic and second,
     Qay' is not specifically mentioned in other sources of
     Islamic law as an act which breaks Wudoo.

c) Conditions for the Acceptance of Hadeeths

Other differences among jurists in the area of the Sunnah arose
from various conditions they placed on its acceptability. For

---

[1] Collected by Muslim (Sahih Muslim (English Trans.), vol. 1, p. 422, no.
1948).

[2] al-Madkhal, p. 210.

[3] Collected by Ibn Maajah from 'Aa'eshah and rated Da'eef (inaccurate) by al-
Albaanee in Da'eef al-Jaami' as-Sagheer (Beirut: al-Maktab al-Islaamee,
1979), vol. 5, p. 167, no. 5434.

example, Imaam Abu Haneefah stipulated that a *Hadeeth* had to be *Mash-hoor* (well known) before being regarded as admissible evidence, whereas Imaam Maalik stipulated that a *Hadeeth* must not contradict the customs of the Madeenites in order to be admissible. On the other hand, Imaam Ahmad considered *Mursal*[1] *Hadeeths* acceptable as proof, while Imaam ash-Shaafi'ee accepted only the *Mursal Hadeeths* of Sa'eed ibn al-Mussayyib which most *Hadeeth* scholars felt were highly authentic.[2]

d) Resolution of Textual Conflict in *Hadeeths*

The founders of the *Madh-habs* and their students took two main approaches in resolving apparent contradictions between the literal meanings of some of the recorded narrations of *Hadeeth*. Some jurists chose the path of *"Tarjeeh"* which meant giving preference to some *Hadeeths* while rejecting others on the same topic. On the other hand, some of the other jurists chose the path of *Jama'*, which involved combining such *Hadeeths* using one in a general sense. For example, there is an authentic *Hadeeth* in which the Prophet (ﷺ) forbade *Salaah* at certain times saying; *"No Salaah (is allowed) after Fajr prayer until the sun has risen and after 'Asr prayer until the sun has set."*[3] At the same time there are other equally authentic *Hadeeths* in which certain *Salaahs* were recommended without

---

[1] *Hadeeth* reported by one of the students of the *Sahaabah* without mentioning the name of the *Sahaabee* from whom he had heard it.

[2] Ibn Taymeeyah, *Raf'ul-Malaam 'an al-A'immah al-A'laam*, (Beirut: al-Maktab al-Islaamee, 3rd. ed., 1970), p. 31.

[3] Reported by 'Umar and Abu Sa'eed al-Khudree and collected by al-Bukhaaree *(Sahih Al-Bukhari* (Arabic-English Trans.), vol. 1, p. 322, no. 555), Muslim *(Sahih Muslim* (English Trans.), vol. 2, p. 395, no. 1805) and Abu Daawood *(Sunan Abu Dawud* (English Trans.), vol. 1, pp. 335-6, no. 1271).

time restriction. For example, *"If any of you enters a masjid, he should pray two Raka'aat (units of prayer) before sitting down."* [1]

(i) Imaam Abu Haneefah gave preference to the first *Hadeeth* and ruled that all forms of *Salaah* were forbidden during the forbidden times.

(ii) Imaam Maalik, Imaam ash-Shaafi'ee and Imaam Ahmad combined the two *Hadeeths,* ruling that the first *Hadeeth* was general and referred to voluntary *Salaah (Nafl),* whereas the second *Hadeeth* was specific, allowing highly recommended *Salaah (Mustahabb)* even during the generally forbidden times. [2]

3. ADMISSIBILITY OF CERTAIN PRINCIPLES

There were among the Imaams some who developed a number of controversial principles on which they based some of their rulings. As a result, both the rulings and the principles became sources of differences among jurists. For example, the majority of jurists recognized the validity of *Ijmaa'* among the generations after the *Sahaabah,* but Imaam ash-Shaafi'ee questioned its occurrence while Imaam Ahmad rejected it outright. Similarly Imaam Maalik's reliance on the customs of the Madeenites as a source of legislation was rejected by the majority of jurists. And, Imaam Abu Haneefah's principle of *Istihsaan* and Maalik's *Istislaah* were both disallowed by Imaam ash-Shaafi'ee as

---

[1] Reported by Abu Qataadah and collected by al-Bukhaaree *(Sahih Al-Bukhari,* (Arabic-English), vol. 1, pp. 259-60, no. 435), Muslim *(Sahih Muslim* (English Trans.), vol. 1, p. 347, no. 1540) and Abu Daawood *(Sunan Abu Dawud* (English Trans.), vol. 1, p. 120, no. 467).

[2] The latter position is supported by the Prophet's (ﷺ) practise of praying missed voluntary prayers of DHuhur after the compulsory prayers of 'Asr which was reported by Umm Salamah and collected by al-Bukhaaree *(Sahih Al- Bukhari* (Arabic-English) vol. 1, p. 325, chapter 33) and Muslim *(Sahih Muslim* (English Trans.), vol. 2, pp. 397-8, no. 1815). See also *Bidaayah al-Mujtahid,* vol. 1, pp. 66-91.

being too independent of the Qur'aan, the Sunnah, and *Ijmaa'*. That is to say, they relied too much, in his opinion, on human reasoning. On the other hand, Imaam ash-Shaafi'ee felt that the opinion of the *Sahaabah* had to be accepted on legal matters, while others felt that it was only reasoning on their part which was not binding on later generations.[1]

4. METHODS OF *QIYAAS*

The various approaches which jurists took in their application of *Qiyaas* were perhaps the largest source of differences among them. Some narrowed down the scope of *Qiyaas* by setting a number of preconditions for its use, while others expanded its scope. Because this principle was based on opinion to a greater extent than any of the others, there were no hard and fast rules with which to contain it, and thus a wide range of differences developed.[2]

Section Summary

1. Varying rulings arose from differences in interpretation which were themselves attributable to variations in word meanings (shared, literal and figurative) and grammatical constructions (e.g. *Qur', Lams* and *elaa*).

2. In the application of *Hadeeths*, a variation of legal rulings occurred depending on the degree of availability of the *Hadeeths*, their authenticity, the conditions imposed for their acceptance and the methods of resolving textual conflicts.

3. Some Imaams evolved certain secondary legal principles and made rulings based on them. Both the principles and the rulings were rejected by other Imaams (e.g. *Istihsaan* and *Ijmaa'* of the Madeenites).

---

[1] *Asbaab Ikhtilaaf al-Fuqahaa*, pp. 126-138. See also *Raf 'ul-Malaam 'anil-A'immah al-A'laam*, pp. 11-49.

[2] *al-Madkhal*, pp. 209-210.

4. The secondary principle of *Qiyaas* was generally accepted, but the rules governing its deductive procedures varied among Imaams, resulting in a variation in their rulings on similar issues.

7 THE FIFTH STAGE: CONSOLIDATION

This stage covers the period between the year 950 CE and the sacking of Baghdad (1258 CE) and represents the decline of the 'Abbaasid dynasty until its eventual collapse. Competitive debates called *MunaadHaraat* continued to flourish under the patronage of the 'Abbaasid caliphs and some of these debates were actually recorded in books. In time, the spirit of rivalry largely generated by these debates spread to the masses, and *Madh-hab* factionalism became widespread. There was a drastic reduction in the number of *Madh-habs*, and the structure and operation of the four that survived became highly systematized. Scholars within a *Madh-hab* were obliged to base their *Ijtihaads* solely on the fundamental principles *(Usool)* of their particular *Madh-hab*. During this period the compilation of *Fiqh* was further formalized and used to further *Madh-hab* rivalry.[1]

Four *Madh-habs*

During this stage, the number of major *Madh-habs* (schools of Islamic law) dwindled to four; three major and one minor. In other words, the *Madh-habs* of great Imaams like al-Awzaa'ee, Sufyaan ath-Thawree, Ibn Abee Laylaa, Abu Thawr and al-Layth ibn Sa'd had all disappeared leaving only the *Madh-habs* of Abu Haneefah, Maalik, ash-Shaafi'ee and Ahmad ibn Hambal. In time, these schools of Islamic legal thought became so predominant that the common people soon forgot that any other schools, even existed. Each of these schools soon took on a dynamism of its own and their followers started the practice of naming themselves after their respective *Madh-habs*. For example, al-Husayn ibn Mas'oud al-Baghawee, author of the *Fiqh* classic, *Sharh as-Sunnah*, was commonly referred to as al-Husayn ibn Mas'oud al-Baghawee ash-Shaafi'ee after the Shaafi'ee *Madh-hab*.

During this stage the scholars of each *Madh-hab* analysed all the rulings of their *Madh-habs'* founding scholars, deduced the fundamental principles behind their rulings and codified them. They also made

---

[1] *al-Madkhal*, pp. 147-157.

limited *Ijtihaads* on issues which the founders had not come across. However, this area soon became exhausted due to the wide-spread use of hypothetical *Fiqh*, in and outside of court debates. Ultimately independent *Ijtihaad* was discarded in favor of *Ijtihaad* based upon the established principles of a particular *Madh-hab*. *Ijtihaad Madh-habee*, as this new form of reasoning came to be known, was based on the deduction of laws for new issues according to the principles laid down by the founders of the particular *Madh-hab*. Thus, the scholars of this period sometimes differed with the founders of their *Madh-habs* with respect to the *Furoo'* (secondary principles), but rarely with regard to the *Usool* (fundamental principles).

The scholars of the *Madh-habs* also made use of the principle of *Tarjeeh* which involved the favoring of certain opinions held by scholars within a given *Madh-hab* over other opinions of that *Madh-hab* on the same topic. Difference of opinion on one issue within a school had arisen when the founding scholars, as well as their students, changed their earlier opinions. Both versions (the previous and the altered) were recorded and passed on to later generations as different opinions of the *Madh-hab*. Differences of opinion had also arisen from different interpretations of statements made by earlier scholars of the *Madh-hab*. In each *Madh-hab*, the scholars during this period of consolidation sifted out weak and fabricated statements which had been attributed to the founders of their respective *Madh-hab*. They also classified the narrations of opinions of the founders according to their accuracy. This process of authentication and classification was referred to as *Tas-heeh*.

This detailed systematic treatment of *Fiqh* within each of the *Madh-habs* greatly facilitated the process of arriving at legal rulings within a *Madh-hab*. However, as in the case of the systematic treatment of the sources of Islamic law in the previous stage, the very fine distinctions elaborated on by the scholars of this period further contributed to *Madh-hab* factionalism.

Compilation of *Fiqh*

During this segment of the 'Abbaasid rule, a format for writing *Fiqh* books evolved. This format became a standard which has remained in practice until today. The various issues were grouped under main headings and the main headings under chapters, each of which represented a major topic from *Sharee'ah*. Even the order of the chapters became standardised. The authors would begin with the four pillars after *Eemaan* (faith), since *Eemaan* was dealt with in books of Islamic theology. After treating the laws and issues concerning *Tahaarah* (hygiene) and *Salaah* (prayer), *Sawm* (fasting), *Zakaah* (poor tax) and *Hajj* (pilgrimage), they would proceed on to *Nikaah* (marriage) and *Talaaq* (divorce), then *Bay'* (business transactions) and then *Aadaab* (etiquette). In dealing with any of these issues, an author from any one *Madh-hab* would mention the different proofs used by all of the *Madh-habs*, then he would end by methodically proving the correctness of his own *Madh-hab's* position, while refuting the arguments of the other *Madh-habs*.

Section Summary

1. The majority of the *Madh-habs* which flourished during the earlier periods disappeared and only four remained.

2. The *Madh-habs* reached their final form of systemization and organization.

3. *Ijtihaad* beyond the structure of the *Madh-hab* was dropped and *Ijtihaad Madh-habee* took its place.

4. Comparative *Fiqh* arose, but was used essentially to advance sectarian ideas.

8 THE SIXTH STAGE: STAGNATION AND DECLINE

This stage covers approximately six centuries starting with the sacking of Baghdad in 1258CE and the execution of the last 'Abbaasid caliph, al-Musta'sim, and ending around the middle of the nineteenth century of the Christian era. This period also represents the rise of the Ottoman Empire, founded in 1299 CE by the Turkish leader 'Uthmaan I, until its decline under the attacks of European colonialism.

The prevailing characteristic of this period was that of *Taqleed* (the blind following of a *Madh-hab*) and factionalism. This degenerative trend resulted in the dropping of all forms of *Ijtihaad* and the evolution of the *Madh-habs* into totally separate entities closely resembling sects. The compilation of *Fiqh* during this period was limited to commenting on previous works and was directed toward the promotion of individual *Madh-habs*. Thus, the dynamism of *Fiqh* was lost and many of the laws became increasingly outmoded and inapplicable in their existing forms. In order to fill this legislative gap, European law codes were gradually introduced in place of some of the Islamic laws which had fallen into disuse. Eventually with the advance of European colonialism and the breaking up of the Muslim empire, Islamic law was supplanted by European laws. Certain reformers sought to stem the tide of stagnation and decline, calling for a return to the original purity of Islaam and its laws. However, factionalism has continued to the present day, in spite of an increase in institutional teaching of comparative *Fiqh*.

Emergence of *Taqleed* [1]

The scholars of this period left all forms of *Ijtihaad* and unanimously issued a legal ruling which was intended to close the door of *Ijtihaad* permanently. They reasoned that all possible issues had already been raised and addressed, and there was therefore no need for further *Ijtihaad*.[2] With that step, a new concept of *Madh-hab* arose, namely

---

[1] The blind following of a *Madh-hab*.

[2] Muhammad Husein adh-Dhahabee, *ash-Sharee'ah al-Islaameeyah*, (Egypt: Daar al-Kutub al-Hadeeth, 2nd ed. 1968), p. 12.

Hanafee
Prayer Place

Maalikee
Prayer Place

Hambalee
Prayer Place

Shaafi'ee
Prayer Place

that one of the four *Madh-habs* had to be followed for one's Islaam to be valid. In time this concept became firmly embedded among the masses as well as the scholars of *Fiqh*. Thus, the religion of Islaam itself became restricted within the confines of the four existing *Madh-habs;* Hanafee, Maalikee, Shaafi'ee and Hambalee. These schools of law came to be considered divinely-ordained manifestations of Islaam. All of them were supposed to be completely correct, equal and representative of true Islaam, yet there were innumerable differences among them. In fact there were scholars in this period who interpreted some *Hadeeths* in such a way as to prove that the Prophet (ﷺ) himself had predicted the appearance of the Imaams and their *Madh-habs*. Consequently, any attempt to go beyond these canonical *Madh-habs* was considered heretical and anyone who refused to follow one of these *Madh-habs* was classified an apostate. The hyperconservative scholars of this stage even went so far as to rule that whoever was caught transferring from one *Madh-hab* to another was liable to punishment at the discretion of the local judge. A ruling was also made in the Hanafee *Madh-hab* prohibiting the marriage of a Hanafee to a Shaafi'ee.[1] And even the second most important pillar of Islaam, *Salaah,* was not spared the effects of *Madh-hab* fanaticism. The followers of the various *Madh-habs* began to refuse to pray behind the Imaams from other *Madh-habs*. This resulted in the building of separate prayer niches in the masjids[2] of communities where more than one *Madh-hab* existed. Masjids of this type can still be seen in places like Syria, where Sunni Muslims follow either the Hanafee or Shaafi'ee *madh-hab*. Even the most holy masjid, *al-Masjid al-Haraam* of Makkah, which represents the unity of Muslims and the religion of Islaam, was affected. Separate prayer niches were set up around the Ka'bah: one for an Imaam from each of the schools. And when the time for *Salaah* came, an Imaam from one of the *Madh-habs* would lead a congregation of followers from his *Madh-hab* in prayer; then another

---

[1] Muhammad Naasir ad-Deen al-Albaanee, *Sifah Salaah an-Nabee,* (Beirut: al-Maktab al-Islaamee ninth ed. 1972), p. 51.

[2] *Masjid* (plural *Masaajid*), the Muslim house of worship.

Imaam from one of the other *Madh-habs* would lead his congregation of followers and so on. It is interesting to note that separate places of prayer for each of the *Madh-habs* remained around the Ka'bah until the first quarter of the twentieth century when 'Abdul-'Azeez ibn Sa'oud and his army conquered Makkah (October of 1924) and united all worshippers behind a single Imaam regardless of his or their *Madh-habs*.

Reasons for *Taqleed*

Taqleed (blind following) has to be distinguished from *Ittibaa'* (reasoned following). The principle of following the rulings of our predecessors is normal and natural. In fact, it is by closely following earlier interpretations of Islaam that the message of Islaam remains uncorrupted through time. For, those early interpretations were founded on the Prophet's (ﷺ) divine inspiration and his divinely guided life style. The Prophet (ﷺ) himself said that the best generation was his generation, then the generation following his, and then the generation following that.[1] However, since Muslims of earlier generations, with the exception of the Prophet (ﷺ), were not infallible, even those earlier interpretations should not be followed <u>blindly</u> - without regard to certain basic principles of reason which enable us to distinguish between right and wrong. In this book the term *Taqleed* (blind following) is used to refer to the actions of those who slavishly follow a single *Madh-hab* regardless of errors that they see. As for the common people who do not have the knowledge to make independent decisions in doubtful situations, it is for them to follow whatever knowledge is available to them, keep their minds open and rely on open-minded scholars as much as possible.

Taqleed was the result of a number of factors, internal and external to the *Madh-habs*, which affected the development of *Fiqh* and the attitude of scholars. No one cause can be singled out as the main cause

---

[1] Reported by Ibn Mas'oud, Abu Hurayrah, 'Imraan ibn Husayn and 'Aa'eshah and collected by Muslim *(Sahih Muslim* (English Trans.), vol. 4, p. 1346, no. 6153 & 6154 and p. 1347, no. 6156 & 6159).

nor can all of the factors be identified. The following are only a few of the more obvious factors which led to this stage of stagnation.

1. The schools of *Fiqh* were completely formed and the minutest of details worked out. The laws for what had occurred, as well as what might occur, were already deduced and recorded due to the extensive development of speculative *Fiqh*. This left little room for *Ijtihaad* and originality. As a result, there developed an overdependence on the works of earlier scholars of the *Madh-habs*.

2. The 'Abbaasid caliphate, which had come to power under the banner of restoring Islamic law to its former place, lost its power to the kings' ministers *(wazeers)*, many of whom were Shi'ites, and the empire eventually broke up into mini-states. The new rulers-by-proxy were more interested in private power struggles than in either religious scholarship or government according to Islamic laws.

3. The crumbling of the 'Abbaasid empire into mini-states was accompanied by each state following the *Madh-hab*, of its choice. For example, Egypt followed the Shaafi'ee *Madh-hab*, Spain the Maalikee *Madh-hab*, and Turkey and India the Hanafee. Each state began the practice of choosing its governors, administrators and judges only from those who followed its official *Madh-hab*. Consequently, scholars who wanted to become *Qaadees* (judges) in the courts of these states had to follow the official *Madh-hab* of the state.

4. Some unqualified individuals began to claim the right to make *Ijtihaad* in order to twist the religion to suit their wishes. Consequently, many incompetent scholars began making rulings which misguided the masses on a number of issues. In the ensuing confusion, the reputable scholars of the day tried to close the door of *Ijtihaad* in order to protect the *Sharee'ah* from being tampered with.[1]

---

[1] *al-Madkhal*, pp. 136-137.

Compilation of *Fiqh*

The same factors which led to *Taqleed* also caused scholars to confine their creative activity to merely editing and revising previous works. The *Fiqh* books of earlier scholars were condensed and abridgements of them were made. These abridgements were later shortened in order to make them easy to memorize, and many of them were actually put to rhyme. This process of condensing continued until the summaries which resulted became virtual riddles to the students of the day. The following generation of scholars began to write explanations of the summaries and poems. Later scholars wrote commentaries on the explanations and others added footnotes to the commentaries.

During this period some books on the fundamentals of *Fiqh (Usool al-Fiqh)* were written. In these works, the correct method of making *Ijtihaad* was outlined and the conditions for its application were clearly defined. However, the conditions which were laid down by these scholars were so strict that they excluded not only the scholars of their time but also many of the earlier scholars who had made *Ijtihaad.*

There were also a few books which were written on comparative *Fiqh* during this period. As in the previous period, the opinions of the *Madh-habs* and their proofs were collected and criticised in these books. The authors then defined as most accurate those opinions which were held by their particular *Madh-hab.*

Toward the end of this period, an attempt was made to codify Islamic law under the auspices of the Ottoman caliphs. A panel of seven top ranking scholars of *Fiqh* was formed and entrusted with the job. It was completed in 1876 CE and enforced as law by the Sultan throughout the Ottoman empire under the title *Majallah al-Ahkaam al-'Aadilah* (The Just Codes)[1]. However, even this seemingly noble attempt was affected by *Madh-hab* fanaticism. All of the scholars on the committee were appointed from the Hanafee *Madh-hab*. Con-

---

[1] Anwar Ahmed Qadri, *Islamic Jurisprudence in the Modern World*, (Lahore, Pakistan: Ashraf, First edition 1963) p. 65.

sequently, the resulting code totally ignored the contributions of the the other *Madh-habs* to *Fiqh*.

With the expeditions of Columbus and Vasco de Gama, Western European states began to capture the routes and sources of international trade. Subsequently, Muslim East Asian states were absorbed by European imperialism beginning with Java which fell to the Dutch in 1684. After Transylvania and Hungary fell from Ottoman hands to Austria in 1699 and the defeat of the Ottomans by Russia in the Russo-Turkish war of 1768-74, the European territories of the Ottoman empire were soon lost, one after another.[1] This process culminated in the total dissolution of the Ottoman Empire during the First World War and its division into colonies and protectorates. Consequently, European law codes replaced Islamic laws throughout the Muslim world.

Although European colonialism was officially ended some years ago, Islamic law has remained in disuse in all Muslim countries with the exception of Saudi Arabia which has codified Islamic law according to the Hambalee *Madh-hab*, Pakistan to a large degree according to the Hanafee *Madh-hab* and Iran which has recently done so according to the Ja'faree *Madh-hab*.[2]

Reformers

In spite of the general decay described above, there existed from time to time throughout this period a few outstanding scholars who opposed *Taqleed* and dared to raise the banner of *Ijtihaad*. They called for a return to the roots of the religion, to the true sources of Islamic law and to reliance on these foundations above all else. Some of these reformers and their contributions are described hereafter.

Ahmad ibn Taymeeyah (1263-1328 CE) was foremost among the reformers of this period. Because of his challenge of the status quo, many of his contemporaries declared him an apostate and had the

---

[1] *Islamic Jurisprudence in the Modern World*, p. 85.

[2] The *Fiqh Madh-hab* of the Ithnaa 'Ashreeyah (Twelver) Shi'ite sect falsely attributed to Imaam Ja'far as-Saadiq (d. 765 CE).

authorities jail him repeatedly. Ibn Taymeeyah was, however, one of the greatest scholars of his time. Initially, he had studied *Fiqh* according to the *Hambalee Madh-hab*, but did not restrict himself to it. He studied the sources of Islamic law in depth and mastered all the Islamic sciences which were known at that time. Furthermore, he examined the writings of various sects which had broken off from Islaam, studied the religious books of the Christians, the Jews and their various sects and wrote extensive critiques on all of them. Ibn Taymeeyah also took part in the *Jihaad* against the Mongols who had occupied the eastern and northern provinces of the former 'Abbaasid state and were at that time threatening Egypt and North Africa. Ibn Taymeeyah's students were among the greatest Islamic scholars of their time and carried on to the next generation the banner of *Ijtihaad* and a return to the pure sources of Islaam which he had raised. Among them was Ibn Qayyim, a great scholar in the fields of *Fiqh* and *Hadeeth*, adh-Dhahabee, a master in the science of *Hadeeth* criticism and Ibn Katheer, a master in *Tafseer*, History and *Hadeeth*.

Muhammad ibn 'Alee ash-Shawkaanee (1757-1835 CE) born near the town of Shawkaan in Yemen, was also among the reformers of this period. Ash-Shawkaanee studied *Fiqh* according to the Zaydee *Madh-hab*[1] and became one of its outstanding scholars. He then went into an in-depth study of the science of *Hadeeth* and subsequently became the most famous scholar of *Hadeeth* of his time. At this point he freed himself of the *Madh-hab* and began making independent *Ijtihaad*. He wrote a number of works in *Fiqh* and its fundamentals in which issues studied from the points of view of all the *Madh-habs* were concluded with solutions based solely on the most accurate proofs and the most convincing arguments. Imaam ash-Shawkaanee took the position that *Taqleed* was *Haraam* and wrote a number of books on the topic, for example, *Al-Qawl al-Mufeed fee Hukm at-Taqleed.* Consequently, he also came under attack from most of the scholars of his time.[2]

---

[1] One of the major *Shi'ite Madh-habs* of *Fiqh* (see pp. 60-65).

[2] Muhammad ibn 'Alee ash-Shawkaanee, *Nayl al-Awtaar*, vol. 1, pp. 3-6.

Another noteworthy reformer was the great scholar Aḥmad ibn 'Abdur-Raḥeem better known as Shah Walee Allaah Dihlawee (1703-1762 CE). He was born in the Indian sub-continent where *Taqleed* was, perhaps, most rampant. After he had mastered the various Islamic sciences, he called for the re-opening of the door of *Ijtihaad* and the re-unification of the schools of *Fiqh*. In his efforts to re-examine Islamic principles and to find out on what authority the legal schools based their regulations, Shah Walee Allaah rejuvenated the study of *Hadeeth*. Although he did not go so far as to reject the existing *Fiqh* schools, nevertheless he taught that everyone was free to choose a particular decision different from that taken by the school to which he belonged himself, if he was convinced that the case was better confirmed by *Hadeeth*.[1]

However the over all state of degeneration and stagnation has continued until today, despite the efforts of modern thinkers like Jamaal ad-Deen al-Afghaanee (1839-1897 CE) who travelled throughout the Muslim world calling for reform. Jamaal ad-Deen travelled to India, Makkah, and Constantinople, settling finally in Egypt. He called for free political, religious and scientific thought and denounced *Taqleed* and state corruption. Jamaal ad-Deen taught these ideas at the University of al-Azhar[2] and influenced many who studied under him. Unfortunately, some of Jamaal ad-Deen's ideas were extremist. For example, he elevated the human mind and its logical deductions to a level equal to that of Divine Revelation. His intentions also became suspect due to his involvement with the Masonic movement which was at that time establishing new branches in the Middle-East.[3]

---

[1] A.J. Arberry, *Religion in the Middle East* (Cambridge University Press, 1969 - reprinted 1981) vol. 2, pp. 128-9.

[2] The oldest and most famous Islamic University in the Muslim world. It was first established in Egypt by the Faaṭimid Shi'ite state in the year 361 AH/972 CE.

[3] Muḥammad Muḥammad Husain, *al-Ittijaahaat al-Waṭaneeyah fee al-Adab al-'Arabee al-Mu'aasir*, vol. 1, p. 153. See also *Religion in the Middle East*, vol. 2, p. 37.

Muhammad 'Abduh (1849-1905 CE) was among Afghaanee's most famous students. Under the influence of Afghaanee and Ibn Taymeeyah's thought, the banner of *Ijtihaad* was again raised high by Muhammad 'Abduh, and *Taqleed* and its supporters were systematically attacked. But, due to Muhammad 'Abduh's leaning toward extreme modernism, he eventually deviated in some of his interpretations and legal rulings. For example, in his *Tafseer* of the Qur'aan he apologetically explained away all of the miracles attributed to the Prophets or directly performed by God through the forces of nature. To him the flocks of birds which dropped clay pebbles on the army of Abrahah and his elephant during their attack on the Ka'bah were simply airborne microbes which spread disease among them. Likewise, he made a *Fatwaa* allowing Muslims to be involved in business transactions involving interest. He based this ruling on the *Fiqh* principle that dire necessity makes the forbidden allowable. The fallacy of his ruling lay in the fact that *Fiqh* specifically defines dire necessity as involving matters of life and death or loss of limb, and this was simply not the case where business transactions are concerned. Muhammad 'Abduh's main student, Muhammad Rasheed Ridaa (d. 1935), carried on his mentor's attack on *Taqleed*, but rejected most of his teacher's excesses. However, other students of Muhammad 'Abduh became the nucleus of the extreme modernist movement and deviated in many areas even more than their teacher. For example, his student Qaasim Ameen (died 1908) was the first to make a vehement attack on polygamy, the simplicity of Islamic divorce and the use of the veil.

Other scholars of the twentieth century, such as Hassan al-Bannaa (d. 1949), founder of the *Ikhwaan Muslimoon* movement Sayyid, Abul-A'laa Mawdudi (1903-1979), founder of the Jama'at Islami movement, and more recently the great *Hadeeth* scholar of our era, Naasir ad-Deen al-Albaanee have picked up the banner of Islamic Revival and have called for the unification of the *Madh-habs*.[1] But, to

---

[1] The book, *Fiqh as-Sunnah*, by as-Sayyid Saabiq, one of al-Bannaa's followers, represents a serious attempt to answer that call.

this day, the majority of scholars remain firmly bound to sectarian Islaam in the form of one of the four *Madh-habs*. In doing so, they unknowingly perpetuate division among the ranks of the Muslim nation. Nor does there appear to be much hope for an end to this process in the near future; for, with very few exceptions, present day Islamic institutions of learning throughout the Muslim world actively propagate a sectarian view of Islaam.

It is true that comparative *Fiqh* is now being given a prominent place in the syllabuses of these institutions, and the study of *Hadeeth* has become more popular than it was only a century ago. But, the reality is that these two potentially dynamic and regenerative subjects have been defused by the sectarian system of Islamic education. Each university adheres to the official *Madh-hab* of the country in which it is situated and thus all the core *Fiqh* courses of the Islamic law syllabus (called *Sharee'ah* or *Usool al-Deen*) are taught according to the state *Madh-hab*[1]. This is done to fulfill the local government's need for judges who conform to the *Madh-hab* used in the civil law system of the state. For example, the University of al-Azhar in Egypt, the most venerated institution in the Muslim world, is the only university in which all of the major *Madh-habs* are taught. However, students entering the university are required to indicate their *Madh-hab* during registration and those of the same *Madh-hab* are placed in the same class. From the beginning of their studies until they graduate, all of their professors will be from their own *Madh-hab*. Accordingly, the positions of the other *Madh-habs* are studied merely as oddities, and the great books of *Hadeeth* are read more for the blessing than for the revelation of truth. Whenever a conflicting opinion is encountered in the course of these studies, the teacher in the sectarian institution examines it superficially and rejects it in the light of the compelling arguments which he develops to support the position of his particular

---

One of the few exceptions to this rule at the present time is the Islamic University of Madeenah, Saudi Arabia. Over 80% of the student body comes from various parts of the Muslim world and no *Madh-hab* is given preference over the other in the study of *Fiqh*, at the college level.

Madh-hab. Thus, although other positions may be supported by very strong proofs, the sectarian teacher's treatment denies them the consideration they deserve. Similarly, if a strong *Hadeeth* which appears contrary to the position taken by the *Madh-hab* is met while reading the books of *Hadeeth*, the teacher either re-interprets it to support his *Madh-hab* or he deftly explains it away. And if neither of the two is possible, a series of weak *Hadeeths* are quoted in support of the *Madh-hab's* position without the slightest mention that they are weak. In that way, it appears that there is a greater number of *Hadeeths* supporting the *Madh-hab's* position, and the students are convinced of the correctness of their *Madh-hab*.

Section Summary

1. *Ijtihaad* in all its forms was put aside, and the blind following *(Taqleed)* of one of the four *Madh-habs* was made compulsory on all Muslims.

2. The four *Madh-habs* became totally incompatible and the Muslim *Ummah* was virtually split into four religious sects.

3. Scholarly activity was restricted to writing commentaries on previous works and promoting the position of the author's particular *Madh-hab* as in the period of consolidation.

4. There were commendable attempts by certain reformers to revive the original and dynamic nature of *Fiqh*, but their efforts proved unequal to the task of eradicating *Madh-hab* fanaticism which had became so deeply ingrained.

5. Attempts at the codification of Islamic law were made, but the results suffered from sectarian views, and with the advent of European colonialism they were supplanted by European law codes.

6. There has been some lessening of *Madh-hab* fanaticism in recent years as a result of the reformist movements and the wide-spread teaching of comparative *Fiqh* in modern institutions of learning.

7. The state of stagnation and decline of *Fiqh* and the existence of *Madh-hab* factionalism have continued until the present day.

9. THE IMAAMS AND TAQLEED

In the preceding chapters we have traced the historical development of *Fiqh* and the *Madh-habs*, showing their interrelationship and their contribution to a general, as well as specific, understanding of Islaam as revealed in the Qur'aan and the Sunnah. It should be noted that both *Fiqh* (Islamic law) and the *Madh-habs* (schools of Islamic thought) were and are necessary additions complementing the divine revelations which define the basic principles governing man's rights and responsibilities in his relationships with Allaah and his fellow man. It is through specific applications of the interpretations of the Qur'aan and the Sunnah that Allaah's divine will can be made manifest to man over time and through space. With God-given intellectual powers man (specifically Islamic scholars) can provide relevant interpretations of the general to meet the particular: thence relevance of the *Madh-hab* (the circle of Islamic scholars) and *Fiqh* (the body of Islamic laws together with principles for deducing these laws). Herein lies the true importance of *Fiqh* and the *Madh-hab* in Islaam.

Now since Islaam is a religion divinely ordained for all men at all times and in all climes, it was given to scholars in different regions and times to evolve principles of *Fiqh* as well as specific laws of *Fiqh* in order to resolve various new issues as they arose. The correctness of their interpretations was proportional to their innate capabilities and to the type and quantity of evidence available to them at the time of making rulings. Some were faced with the additional factor of cultural differences, and many were deprived of the assistance to be gained from mutual consultation, owing to their distance from their colleagues and the consequent difficulties of communication. Hence the differences of opinion that arose from region to region. Despite various handicaps, the early scholars discharged their duties to Islaam and to their fellowmen by using their God-given powers of intellect to interpret Allaah's purposes for man. Situated in different parts of the Muslim state, they became the founders of different schools of Islamic thought, hence the multiplication of *Madh-habs* at one stage in the evolution of the Islamic law and the Muslim state. Historically, therefore, the appearance of more than one *Madh-hab* was inevitable. Furthermore, as the numbers of *Madh-habs* increased and communication and other factors exercised their influence, difference and contradictions, too, were a natural outcome. However, so long as scholars managed to keep the goal of truth foremost in mind and were not led astray by sectarianism, fanaticism, or a desire for personal glory and reward, the essential spirit of Islaam was preserved in their *Madh-habs*. In such circumstances, scholars were in no way reluctant to abandon their individual opinions in favour of rulings by others which were clearly shown to be nearer the intended meaning deducible from the Qur'aan and the Sunnah. In other words, there was a continuing search for truth up until such time as the negative factors previously mentioned (sectarianism and desire for personal glory) became dominant in the lives of some of the scholars. Then, indeed, blind following of a *Madh-hab (Taqleed)* coupled with the ban on *Ijtihaad* led to the widespread promotion of sectarianism among the masses and the general decline in the search for truth among many scholars. Thereafter, the four surviving *Madh-habs*, with their different and sometimes contradictory rulings, assumed the character of infallibility, and spurious *Hadeeths* arose to bolster this anti-Islamic trait. As a counter to this decline, various reform movements through the ages have called for a unification of the *Madh-habs* or, in some cases, rejection of the need for any *Madh-hab*. The former position is a legitimate one, as we have shown; the latter is an extremist one, possibly heretical since it overlooks the importance of a unified school of Islamic thought as a necessary complement to the Qur'aan and the Sunnah, for a better understanding and appreciation of Allaah's divine laws.

From the historical development of *Fiqh* and the evolution of the *Madh-habs* described in the preceding chapters, we have seen that there was a period during which natural differences among the various *Madh-habs* became extremely exaggerated to the point of sectarianism, so much so that scholars of that time discarded *Ijtihaad* and imposed upon the generality of Muslims the blind following *(Taqleed)* of one of the four major *Madh-habs*. However, the Imaams to whom the four schools are attributed were themselves totally against the enshrinement of these differences and fought vehemently against *Taqleed* either among their own followers or among the masses in general. Yet, till today, many people feel that if an authentic *Hadeeth* should be discarded because, accepting it would mean declaring that the Imaam of one's *Madh-hab* was mistaken in his ruling which, in their opinion is an act of disrespect akin to blasphemy. Little do they realize that their preference of their Imaam's opinion over the Prophet's (ﷺ) statement is itself in total opposition to the stand taken by their own Imaam, and is in fact bordering on a form of *Shirk*[1] known as *"Shirk fee Tawheed al-Ittibaa'"*, that is sharing the unquestioned following which belongs only to the Prophet (ﷺ). For in the declaration of one's Islaam (there is no god but Allaah and Muhammad is the messenger of Allaah), the Prophet (ﷺ) is accepted as being the only person who should be followed unquestioningly, since following him is equivalent to following Allaah.

As most Muslims today are unaware of the contradiction between the position of the early Imaams and that of their *Madh-hab* as it exists today, it is appropriate here to take a closer look at the stand taken by the early Imaams and their students towards *Taqleed* as revealed in their actual statements.

Imaam Abu Haneefah Nu'maan ibn Thaabit (702-767 CE)

Abu Haneefah used to discourage his students from recording his opinions, since they were often based on *Qiyaas* (analogical deduction). However, he made an exception of those opinions which were throughly debated and agreed upon by all his students. His student, Abu Yoosuf, reported that the Imaam once told him, *"Woe be on you, Ya'qoob. Do not write down all you hear from me, for surely I may hold an opinion today and leave it tomorrow, hold another tomorrow and leave it the day after."*[2] This attitude of the Imaam kept his stu-

---

[1] Association of other gods with Allaah (i.e. idolatry).
[2] Reported by 'Abbaas and Ad-Dooree in *at-Taareekh* by Ibn Mu'een (Makkah: King 'Abdul Aziz University, 1979), vol. 6, p. 88.

dents from blind imitation of his views, and helped to develop in them a respect for their own opinions as well as that of others.

Imaam Abu Ḥaneefah also made many strong statements concerning the blind following of his opinions and those of his students. In fact he strictly forbade anyone from following their opinions or making legal rulings based on them unless such a person was familiar with the proofs which he and his students had used and the sources from whence they had deduced them. The Imaam was reported by his student Zufar to have said, *"It is forbidden for anyone who does not know my proofs to make a ruling according to my statements, for verily we are only humans we may say something today and reject it tomorrow."* [1]

Abu Haneefah was always aware of his limitations. Accordingly, he defined for his students and all who would benefit from his deep understanding of Islaam that the ultimate criterion for right and wrong was the Qur'aan and the Sunnah; what was in accordance with them was right and what was not was wrong. His student, Muḥammad ibn al-Hasan, reported that he said, *"If I have made a ruling which contradicts Allaah's book or the messenger's (ﷺ) Ḥadeeth, reject my ruling."* [2] It is also recorded that he pointed out the fact that the principle to follow, if one wanted to follow his *Madh-hab* as he intended it to be followed, is the acceptance of sound *Ḥadeeth.* Imaam Ibn 'Abdul-Barr reported that Imaam Abu Ḥaneefah said, *"If a **Ḥadeeth** is found to be Ṣaḥeeḥ (authentic), it is my Madh-hab."* [3]

Imaam Maalik Ibn Anas (717-801CE)

Imaam Maalik never hesitated to change his rulings, even if he had already uttered them in public, if proof to the contrary came to him

---

[1] Ibn 'Abdul-Barr, *al-Intiqaa fee Fadaa'il ath-Thalaathah al-A'immah al-Fuqahaa,* (Cairo: Maktab al-Qudsee, 1931), p. 145.

[2] Al-Fulaanee, *Eeqaadh al-Himam,* (Cairo: al-Muneereeyah, 1935), p. 50.

[3] Ibn 'Aabideen, *al-Haashiyah,* (Cairo: al-Muneereeyah, 1833-1900), vol. 1, p. 63.

from a reliable source. One of his main students, Ibn Wahb confirmed this attitude of the Imaam saying, "*I once heard someone ask Maalik about washing between the toes during* **Wudoo,** *to which he replied, 'People do not have to do it.' I waited until most of the people left the study circle and informed him that there is a* **Hadeeth** *concerning it. He asked what it was, so I said, that al-Layth ibn Sa'd, Ibn Luhay'ah and 'Amr ibn Al-Ḥaarith all related from al-Mustawrid ibn Shidaad al-Qurashee that he saw Allaah's Messenger ( ) rub between his toes with his little finger, Maalik said, 'Surely that is a good* **Hadeeth** *which I have never heard before.' Later When I heard people ask Maalik about washing between the toes, he used to insist that it must be washed.*" [1] This narration is clear proof that Maalik's *Madh-hab*, like Abu Ḥaneefah's was that of the *sound Hadeeth,* even though we do not have a specific statement by him to that effect, as in the case of Abu Ḥaneefah.

Maalik also emphasized the fact that he was subject to error and that the only rulings of his which should be used were those which did not come in conflict with the Qur'aan and *Hadeeth*. Ibn 'Abdul-Barr reported that Maalik once said, "*Verily I am only a man, I err and am at times correct; so thoroughly investigate my opinions, then take whatever agrees with the Book and the Sunnah, and reject whatever contradicts them.*" [2] This statement clearly proves that the Qur'aan and the *Hadeeth* were given preference over all else by this great scholar who never intended that his opinions be rigidly followed. In fact, when the 'Abbaasid Caliphs Abu Ja'far al-Manṣoor (reign 759-755 CE) and Haroon ar-Rasheed (reign 786-809 CE) requested that Maalik allow them to make his collection of *Hadeeths*, called **al-Muwaṭṭa'**, the official authority in the state on the Sunnah, he refused on both occasions, pointing out that the *Saḥaabah* had scattered throughout the land and

---

[1] Ibn Abee Ḥaatim, *al-Jarḥ wat-Ta'deel*, (Hyderabad, India: Majlis Daa'irah al-Ma'aarif al-'Uthmaaneeyah, 1952), foreword pp. 31-33.

[2] Ibn 'Abdul-Barr, *Jaami' Bayaan al-Ilm*, (Cairo: al-Muneereeyah, 1927), vol. 2, p. 32.

had left behind many *Hadeeths* not found in his collection. Thus, Maalik turned down the opportunity to have his *Madh-hab* made the official *Madh-hab* of the Islamic state and in so doing, he set an example that others might have been wise to follow.

Imaam ash-Shaafi'ee (767-820 CE)

Imaam ash-Shaafi'ee, like his teacher Maalik, pointed out in no uncertain terms that it was not possible for anyone at that time [1] to be aware of all the *Hadeeths* which were narrated from the Prophet (ﷺ) or to remember all *Hadeeths* which he had encountered, therefore, they were bound to make some wrong judgements. That meant that the only firm and reliable method, which could be utilized under all circumstances to decide what was correct and what was not, was the Sunnah of the Prophet (ﷺ). The *Hadeeth* scholar al-Haakim collected a statement of ash-Shaafi'ee in which he said, *"There is no one among us who has not had a Sunnah of Allaah's messenger (ﷺ) elude him or have one slip his mind; so no matter what rulings I have made or fundamental principles I have proposed, there will be in them things contrary to rulings of Allaah's messenger (ﷺ). Therefore, the correct ruling is according to what Allaah's messenger (ﷺ) said, and that is my ruling."* [2]

The Imaam also stressed a very important point concerning personal opinion versus the Sunnah. He said, *"The Muslims (of my time) were of a unanimous opinion that one who comes across an authentic Sunnah of Allaah's messenger (ﷺ) is not allowed to disregard it in favor of someone else's opinion."* [3] This point strikes at the very heart

---

[1] The main collections of *Hadeeth* like that of al-Bukhaaree, Muslim and the others belong to the latter half of the 9th century CE.

[2] Ibn 'Asaakir, *Taareekh Dimishq al-Kabeer*, (Damascus: Rawdah ash-Shaam, 1911-1932), vol. 15, part 1, p. 3.

Ibn al-Qayyim, *I'laam al-Mooqi'een*, (Beirut: Daar al-Jeel n.d.), vol. 2, p. 361.

of *Taqleed* which has as one of its pillars the rejection of the Sunnah for the opinion of the *Madh-hab*.

Al-Haakim also collected from Imaam ash-Shaafi'ee the same statement made by Imaam Abu Haneefah concerning the relationship between his *Madh-hab* and authentic *Hadeeths*, *"If a **Hadeeth** is found to be **Saheeh** (authentic) it is my **Madh-hab**."*[1] Such was the uncompromising stand of this great Imaam who, while in Baghdad, wrote a book called **al-Hujjah** as a summary of his *Madh-hab,* only to turn around and write a new book called **al-Umm**, representing the new *Madh-hab* which he formed after journeying to Egypt and acquiring new knowledge from the *Madh-hab* of Imaam al-Layth ibn Sa'd.

Imaam Ahmad ibn Hambal (778-855 CE)

Imaam Ahmad carried on the tradition of his teacher, Imaam ash-Shaafi'ee as well as that of the earlier Imaams by trying to instill in his students a high respect for the sources of Islaam and a disdain for rigid imitation of scholars' opinions. But, because *Taqleed* had begun to take root among some of the followers of the earlier Imaams, Ahmad took even more drastic action. Whereas Abu Haneefah discouraged his students from recording all of his opinions, Imaam Ahmad forbade them from recording any of his opinions at all. Thus, his *Madh-hab* was not compiled in written form until the era of his students.

Ahmad was very explicit in his warnings against *Taqleed*, as is evident in the following saying of his recorded by Ibn Qayyim: *"Do not blindly follow my rulings, those of Maalik, ash-Shaafi'ee, al-Awzaa'ee, or ath-Thawree. Take (your rulings) from whence they took theirs."*[2] Similarly, in another of his statements recorded by Ibn 'Abdul-Barr, he said, *"The opinions of al-Awzaa'ee, Maalik and Abu Haneefah are*

---

[1] Yahyaa ibn Sharaf ad-Deen an-Nawawee, *al-Majmoo'* (Cairo: Idaarah at-Tabaa'ah al-Muneerah, 1925), vol. 1, p. 63.

[2] *Eeqaadh al-Himam*, p. 113.

simply opinions and to me they are all equal, but the real criterion for right or wrong is in the Ḥadeeths." [1]

The Imaam's preference for *Hadeeths* over opinions was so great that he used to prefer a weak *Hadeeth* over a deduced ruling. His respect for the Sunnah of the Prophet (ﷺ), which he himself collected in a major work of over 30,000 *Hadeeths* called **al-Musnad Al-Kabeer,** was so great that he also gave severe warnings to those who would dare disregard a *Hadeeth* of the Prophet (ﷺ). Ibn al-Jawzee reported that Imaam Aḥmad said, *"Whoever rejects an authentic Ḥadeeth of Allaah's messenger (ﷺ) is on the verge of destruction."* [2] The Prophet (ﷺ) had given the following order to his companions and Muslims in general: *"Convey what you have heard from me, even if it is only a verse (from the Qur'aan),"* [3] in order that divine guidance would be available to all generations of Muslims until the Last Day. Because of that, Imaam Aḥmad fought vigilantly against anything which could possibly interfere with the conveyance of divine guidance to his generation as well as those to come.

Students of the Imaams

Because of the care which the great Imaams took in warning their students away from blind imitation, those early scholars never hesitated to reject what the Imaams taught when new *Hadeeths* became available. Abu Yoosuf and Muḥammad ibn al-Ḥasan differed from their teacher Abu Ḥaneefah in about one third of the rulings of their *Madh-hab,* [4] and similarly, al-Muzanee and the others differed from their teacher ash-Shaafi'ee on many rulings.

---

[1] *Jaami Bayaan al-'Ilm,* vol. 2, p. 149.

[2] ibn al-Jawzee, *al-Manaaqib,* (Beirut: Daar al-Aafaaq al-Jadeedah, 2nd ed., 1977). p. 182.

[3] Narrated by 'Abdullaah ibn 'Amr ibn al-'Aas and collected by al-Bukhaaree *(Sahih Al-Bukhari,* (Arabic-English), vol. 4, p. 442, no. 667).

[4] *al-Haashiyah,* vol. 1, p. 62.

Comment

The above mentioned quotations were only a few of the many sayings of the Four Imaams and their students in which they demanded strict adherence to the *Hadeeths* and prohibited the blind imitation of their opinions, may Allaah be pleased with them. Their statements are perfectly clear and leave no room for misinterpretation or apologetic explanations. Therefore, whoever adheres to the Sunnah, even if he finds himself in conflict with some of the opinions of the Imaam of his *Madh-hab* will not be opposed to the spirit of that *Madh-hab*, but will be following all of the *Madh-habs* simultaneously with a firm grip "on the rope of Allaah". Conversely, to discard certain reliable *Hadeeths* simply because they contradict some of the opinions of the Imaams, is to be in total opposition to the position taken by the Imaams themselves. Moreover, the rejection of reliable *Hadeeths* is in opposition to Allaah and His messenger[1] as is evident in Allaah's statement in the Qu'raan to His Prophet (ﷺ).

فَلَا وَرَبِّكَ لَا يُؤْمِنُونَ حَتَّىٰ يُحَكِّمُوكَ فِيمَا شَجَرَ بَيْنَهُمْ ثُمَّ لَا يَجِدُوا فِي أَنفُسِهِمْ حَرَجًا مِّمَّا قَضَيْتَ وَيُسَلِّمُوا تَسْلِيمًا

"No, by your Lord, they do not believe until they make you the judge between them in their disputes without being distressed over your judgement; nay, accepting it wholeheartedly."[2]

---

[1] Muhammad Naasir ad-Deen al-Albaanee, *Sifah Salaah an-Nabee*, foreword pp. 34-35.

[2] Soorah an-Nisaa (4):65.

For example, Imaam Muhammad ibn al-Hasan in his narration of Imaam Maalik's book, *al-Muwatta*, contradicted his teacher Imaam Abu Haneefah in about 20 different rulings. Among them was the following case in which Imaam Muhammad said, *"Abu Haneefah did not feel that there was any ordained Salaah (prayer) for* **Istisqaa**,[1] *but in my opinion, the Imaam should lead the people in two units of Salaah, (for Istisqaa) make a* **Du'aa**[2] *and reverse his cloak,"*[3] Another example is that of the inheritance of the grandfather if the father of the dead person is also dead. Abu Yoosuf and Muhammad both rejected Abu Haneefah's position and joined the position of the other three Imaams, giving the grandfather a sixth of the inheritance which would have gone to the father were he alive.

'Isaam ibn Yoosuf al-Balakhee, who was a student of Imaam Muhammad ibn al-Hasan and a close follower of Abu Yoosuf, used to make a lot of rulings which differed from those of Abu Haneefah and his two companions, because the latter were not aware of certain evidence which later became available to him.[4] For example, he used to raise his hands before and after *Rukoo'* (bowing in *Salaah*),[5] as described in authentic *Hadeeths* by a host of *Sahaabah*, even though the three main Imaams of his *Madh-hab* ruled otherwise.

Allaah also went on to warn those who reject the Sunnah of His

---

[1] Prayer for rain in times of drought.

[2] Informal prayer.

[3] Muhammad ibn al-Hasan, *at-Ta'leeq al-Mumajjid 'Alaa Muwatta' Muhammad*, p. 158, quoted in *Sifah Salaah an-Nabee*, p. 38.

[4] Ibn 'Aabideen, *Rasm al-Muftee*, vol. 1, p. 27, quoted in *Sifah Salaah an-Nabee*, p. 37.

[5] *Al-Fawaa'id al-Baahiyah fee Taraajim al-Hanafiyah*, p. 116, quoted in *Sifah Salaah an-Nabee*, foreword, p. 39.

Prophet (ﷺ), saying,

فَلْيَحْذَرِ الَّذِينَ يُخَالِفُونَ عَنْ أَمْرِهِ أَن تُصِيبَهُمْ فِتْنَةٌ أَوْ يُصِيبَهُمْ
عَذَابٌ أَلِيمٌ

**"Let those who contradict your order be warned that they
will be afflicted with trials and a painful punishment."** [1]

Nevertheless, the prohibition of *Taqleed* does not mean that
everyone must return to the sources before doing anything and it does
not mean that all the work of the earlier scholars should be rejected or
neglected, for that would be impractical and in most cases impossible.
It does, however, mean that those who have sufficient knowledge of
the various branches of Islamic sciences should not hesitate to look at
the sources as well as the opinions of all the scholars, regardless of
their *Madh-hab*. A scholar should be open-minded in his search for
knowledge otherwise his rulings are likely to be biased and sectarian.
Let us not forget that even in searching through the sources he is
obliged to rely on the great works of the earlier scholars in one way or
another. In *Fiqh*, totally independent thought is impossible and efforts
to achieve it undesirable, as it tends to lead to deviation and heresy.
On any particular issue the true scholar is likely to either follow a ruling of one or another of the early scholars, or deduce his ruling from one of
their deductions. In so doing, he will be following one of the early
Imaams directly or indirectly. However, this form of following is not
to be considered *Taqleed*, (blind rigid imitation), which we have
shown was forbidden categorically by the Imaams. This form is called
Ittibaa' wherein reliable *Hadeeths* take precedence over all opinions,
or as both Abu Haneefah and ash-Shaafi'ee said, *"If the **Hadeeth** is
found to be Saheeh, it is my Madh-hab"*.

It is obvious that the great majority of Muslims will not be able to
return to the sources, due to their lack of knowledge, and they will
therefore be obliged to apply *Ittibaa'* to the degree of their ability.

---

[1] Soorah an-Noor (24):63.

-127-

Many can achieve an awareness of the relevant *Hadeeths* by asking questions concerning the basis for rulings given to them and reading the books of *Hadeeth*. No true scholar should be offended by such questions if politely worded. Similarly, if the masses are forced to seek answers from books, they should try to choose books which mention explanations and proofs along with the various rulings, and books which are not biased or sectarian. If such books are not readily available, then they may still avoid *Taqleed* by not restricting themselves to the books of one *Madh-hab*. As long as they are prepared to follow the Sunnah, whenever it is presented to them, regardless of which *Madh-hab* it may be found in, they are in effect practicing *Ittibaa‘*, not *Taqleed*.

Section Summary

1. Most Muslims are unaware of the fact that blind following of a *Madh-hab (Taqleed)* is diametrically opposed to the position and teachings of the founders of the *Madh-habs*.

2. All of the Imaams and their students were on record as being opposed to the blind following of their opinions. Instead they repeatedly emphasized the importance of referring to the primary sources, the Qur'aan and the Sunnah, as the basis of legal rulings.

3. The Imaams and their students continuously emphasized the fact that their rulings were subject to error.

4. Authentic *Hadeeths* were given precedence by the Imaams over their own opinions. On the basis of authentic *Hadeeths* not available to the Imaams, their students later overruled several rulings previously made by the Imaams.

5. Giving preference to the opinion of a *Madh-hab* over an authentic *Hadeeth* borders on *Shirk* since such preference contravenes the allegiance owed to Allaah and His chosen messenger.

6. All Muslims are required to follow with reason *(Ittibaa‘)* the rulings of the early scholars in order to preserve the pristine purity of Islaam as revealed to the Prophet (ﷺ) and conveyed to his companions.

10 DIFFERENCES AMONG THE UMMAH

In the preceding chapters the writer has endeavoured to trace and account for the historical development of *Madh-habs,* schools of Islamic legal thought, and to show their overall contributions to the progressive enrichment and unifying character of *Fiqh* within the Muslim world. It has been amply demonstrated that the liberal thinking which characterized the early Imaams and their *Madh-habs,* from the time of the Prophet (ﷺ) down through the ages, has been steadily replaced by a certain rigidity and dogmatism. Since the late thirteenth century, not only have the *Madh-habs* become spawning grounds of sectarianism, but *Fiqh* has lost its original vitality which was enshrined in the principle of *Ijtihaad* and thus it has not been able to keep pace with changing circumstances. As a result of *Madh-hab* sectarianism and *Fiqh* inflexibility, the traditional purity, unity and dynamism of Islaam have been threatened throughout the Muslim world.

In this final chapter the writer will examine the phenomenon of **differences and disagreement** *(Ikhtilaaf)* in the light of the positions of early scholars and their students. He will also endeavour to reinforce the fact that while differences of opinion are inevitable, unreasoning disagreement and sectarianism have no place in the religion of Islaam which Allaah in His wisdom revealed to His Prophet (ﷺ).

In treating the historical development (and evolution) of the *Madh-habs* and the concurrent growth of *Fiqh* into a full-fledged Islamic science, we have seen that the great Imaams and founders of the *Madh-habs* generally adopted the stand that:

(a) *Madh-habs* singly or in their totality were not infallible and

(b) the following of any one *Madh-hab* was not obligatory for Muslims.

Yet the pervasive influence of *Taqleed* has resulted, among other things, in a complete turnabout, so much so, that for centuries now the position taken by the generality of Muslims is that the four *Madh-habs* are divinely ordained and therefore infallible; the legal rulings of each of those *Madh-habs* are all sound and correct; everyone must follow one of the four *Madh-habs;* a Muslim should not change his or her *Madh-hab;* and it is wrong to pick and choose rulings across *Madh-habs*. As a corollary to these beliefs, it has been stated that anyone who dares openly to deny the infallibility of all four *Madh-habs* or the obligation to follow one of these *Madh-habs* is considered an *accursed innovator and apostate.*

In the 20th century the most commonly used epithet for describing such an apostate has been the label *Wahhabi* (pronounced Wahhaabee). Another similarly abusive term which is used mostly in India and Pakistan is *Ahl-i-Hadeeth,* Incidentally, both of these terms are in reality misnomers, as the following explanatory comments will reveal.

In the years 1924-25 the followers of Muhammad ibn 'Abdul-Wahhaab (1703-1787) zealously destroyed all structures built over graves of the *Sahaabah* and other revered persons in the cemeteries of the holy cities of Makkah and Madeenah. The so called *Wahhabis* were also opposed to *Tawassul* (seeking intercession from the dead), which had become a widespread practice among the masses of Muslims as well as among many scholars. Since *Tawassul* and the attachment to monuments and shrines had long been ingrained in the Muslim world, the destructive act of the *Wahhabis* in 1924-25 appeared to be innovative and extremist; hence the application of the epithet *Wahhabi* to "accursed innovators" and "apostates". It should be noted, however, that Ibn 'Abdul-Wahhaab, founder of the *Wahhabi* movement, followed the *Fiqh* of the Hambalee *Madh-hab* and that his present-day followers continue to do so.

Furthermore, in opposing *Tawassul* and destroying monuments and shrines to the dead, the twentieth-century descendants and followers of Ibn 'Abdul-Wahhaab were attacking anti-Islamic practices. The Prophet (ﷺ) had ordered the demolition of all idols and statues, and the levelling of all tombs with the surrounding earth, according to an authentic *Hadeeth* reported by 'Alee ibn Abee Taalib and collected by the great *Hadeeth* scholar Muslim ibn Hajjaaj.[1] From the above it

---

[1] *Sahih Muslim* (English Trans.), vol. 2, p. 459, no. 2115. See also *Sunan Abu* =

should now be clear that the word *Wahhabi* applied to mean "accursed innovator" and "apostate" is in fact a mislabel.

Similarly, the term *Ahl-i-Hadeeth (Ar. Ahl al-Hadeeth)* was a title of respect and praise given to scholars in the past who like Imaam Maalik, devoted much time and effort to the specialized study of *Hadeeth.*Towards the end of the nineteenth century this title was adopted by a reform movement in India and Pakistan which called for a return to the Qur'aan and the *Hadeeth* as the basis of *Fiqh* and which opposed the dogmatic adherence to *Madh-habs*. However, present day *Madh-hab* fanaticism and sectarianism have distorted the meaning of the term *Ahl-i-Hadeeth* to apply to one who fanatically opposes the following of any of the *Madh-habs*.

The irony is that, in light of our insight into the historical evolution of the *Madh-habs* and concurrent development of *Fiqh*, the true deviants from the teachings of Islaam are not the so-called *Wahhabi* and *Ahl-i-Hadeeth*, but those people who would rigidly insist on every Muslim following one or another of the four *Madh-habs* and on their believing blindly in the infallibility of all four *Madh-habs*, despite certain glaring contradictions in their rulings on points of Islamic law. Yet it must be acknowledged that those who advocate blind following *(Taqleed)*, are often very sincere in their belief in the infallibility of all four *Madh-habs*. Furthermore many scholars are included in their ranks.[1]

Dawud (English Trans.), vol. 2, pp. 914-5, no. 3212. The text of the *Hadeeth* is narrated by Abu al-Hayyaaj al-Asadee who reported that 'Alee ibn Abee Taalib said to him *"Shall I send you as the Messenger of Allaah sent me? To deface every statue or picture in houses and **level all elevated graves**."*

---

[1] Under the heading **Taqleed Restricted to the Four Mathā-hib,** the author of *Taqleed and Ijtihād* writes: "It was realized from the exposition of the *Wujūb* of *Taqleed* that adoption of different verdicts leads to anarchy. It is therefore, imperative to make *Taqleed* of *Math-hab* which has been so formulated and arranged in regard to principles *(Uṣūl)* and details *(Furū')* that answers to all questions could be obtained....thereby obviating the need to refer to an

How then do those who insist on *Taqleed* reconcile the known differences and contradictions from *Madh-hab* to *Madh-hab* with their belief in the infallibility of all four *Madh-habs*? Some of them claim that the *Madh-habs* were divinely ordained and the Prophet (ﷺ) himself prophesied their coming. Most often, however, they rest their case, mainly on the evidence of the following *Hadeeths*:

$$ اِخْتِلَافُ أُمَّتِى رَحْمَةٌ $$

(a) *"Disagreement among my nation is a mercy."*

(b) *"Differences among my Sahaabah are a mercy for you."*[1]

$$ أَصْحَابِي كَالنُّجُومِ بِأَيِّهِمْ اِقْتَدَيْتُمْ اِهْتَدَيْتُمْ $$

(c) *"My Sahaabah are like stars. You will be guided by whichever of them you follow."*[2]

(d) *"Verily my Sahaabah are like stars. You will be guided by any statement of theirs you adopt."*[3]

(e) *"I asked my Lord about the things in which my companions will differ after my death and Allaah revealed to me: 'Oh Muhammad,*

= external source. This all-embracing quality, by an act of Allaah *Ta'ala,* is found existing in only the four *Mathā-hib. It is therefore, imperative to adopt one of four Mathā-habs."* Maulana Muhammad Maseehullah Khan Sherwani's *Taqleed and Ijtihād* (Port Elizabeth, South Africa: The Majlis, 1980), published by Majlisul Ulama of South Africa. p. 13.

----

[1] Allegedly reported by Jaabir and collected by al-Bayhaqee.

[2] Allegedly reported by Ibn 'Umar and collected by Ibn Battah in *al-Ibaanah,* Ibn 'Asaakir, and NidHaam al-Mulk in *al-Amaalee,* quoted in *Silsilah al-Ahaadeeth ad-Da'eefah wa al-Mawdoo'ah,* (Beirut: al-Maktab al-Islaamee, 3rd ed., 1972), vol. 1, p. 82.

[3] Allegedly reported by Ibn 'Abbaas and collected by al-Khateeb al-Baghdaadee in *al-Kifaaayah fee 'Ilm ar-Riwaayah,* (Cairo: Daar al-Kutub al-Hadeethah, 2nd. ed., 1972).

verily to Me, your companions are like stars in the sky, some brigh-
ter than others. So he who follows anything over which they (the
Ṣaḥaabah) have differed, as far as I am concerned, he will be fol-
lowing guidance'." [1]

However, before these *Ḥadeeths* can be accepted as evidence for sectarianism, they must be clearly shown to be authentic. An examination
of these *Ḥadeeths* has indeed been made by eminent scholars and their
conclusions are recorded hereafter.

As for the *Ḥadeeths* in which the Prophet (ﷺ) was supposed to
have foretold the coming of the Imaams and their *Madh-habs*, the
authentic ones are all generally worded with no specific mention of
either the names of the Imaams or their *Madh-habs*, while those
Ḥadeeths that are specifically worded are all fabricated. [2]

With regard to *"Ḥadeeth"* (a) above, it has no chain of narration
connecting it to anyone, much less to the Prophet (ﷺ); nor is it to be

---

[1] Allegedly reported by Ibn 'Umar and collected by Ibn Baṭṭah in *al-Ibaanah*,
Ibn 'Asaakir, and NidHaam al-Mulk in *al-Amaalee* and quoted in *Silsilah al-
Ahaadeeth aḍ-Ḍa'eefah*, vol. 1, pp. 80-81.

[2] For example al-Khaṭeeb collected a *Ḥadeeth* attributed to the Prophet
(ﷺ) through Abu Hurayrah in which he was supposed to have said, *"There
will be among my Ummah a man called Abu Ḥaneefah, he will be the lamp of
my Ummah."* Al-Khaṭeebs himself and al-Ḥaakim declared it *Mawdoo'*
(forged), among the fabrications of Muhammad ibn Sa'eed al-Marwazee
(Muhammad ibn 'Alee ash-Shawkaanee, *al-Fawaa'id al-Majmoo'ah*,
(Beirut: al-Maktab al-Islaamee, 2nd ed., 1972), p. 320, no. 1226). Al-
Khaṭeeb collected another report through Anas in which the Prophet (ﷺ)
was quoted as saying, *"There will come after me a man called an-Nu'maan ibn
Thaabit, pet-named Abu Ḥaneefah. Allaah's religion and my Sunnah will be
revived by him."* It has in its chain of narrators Ahmad al-Juwaybaaree, a
known fabricator of *Ḥadeeths* and Muhammad ibn Yazeed as-Salamee,
whose narrations are classified unacceptable *(Matrouk)* by *Ḥadeeth* scholars. ('Alee ibn 'Iraaq, *Tanzeeh ash-Sharee'ah al-Marfoo'ah* (Beirut: Daar al-
Kutub al-'Ilmeeyah, 1979), vol. 2, p. 30, no. 10).

found in any of the books of *Hadeeth*.[1] It is therefore incorrect to even refer to it as a *Hadeeth*, as it is fabricated. With regard to "*Hadeeths*" (b) to (e) above, although they can be found in books of *Hadeeth* or about *Hadeeth*, they have all proven to be unauthentic. The first is classified by *Hadeeth* scholars as *Waahin* (extremely weak)[2], the second and third as *Mawdoo'* (fabricated)[3] and the fourth as *Baatil* (false).[4] Thus, the *Hadeeth* evidence for the glorification and perpetuation of differences among *Madh-habs*, is totally unacceptable from the point of view of authenticity.

Not only are these so-called *Hadeeths* unauthentic, but their very meanings are in obvious conflict with the Qur'aan itself. Throughout the Qur'aan's one hundred and fourteen chapters, Allaah has clearly cursed and forbidden religious disagreement and has ordered unity and agreement. Disagreement has been explicitly forbidden in verses such as:

وَلَا تَنَازَعُوا فَتَفْشَلُوا وَتَذْهَبَ رِيحُكُمْ

"Do not dispute among yourselves and cause your own failure and loss of power"[5]

and

وَلَا تَكُونُوا مِنَ الْمُشْرِكِينَ ۩ مِنَ الَّذِينَ فَرَّقُوا دِينَهُمْ
وَكَانُوا شِيَعًا كُلُّ حِزْبٍ بِمَا لَدَيْهِمْ فَرِحُونَ

"Do not be like those among the idolaters who split up their religion into sects, each group happy with what they had".[6]

---

[1] Narrated by al-Manaawee from the great *Hadeeth* scholar as-Subkee.

[2] *Silsilah al-Ahaadeeth ad-Da'eefah wa al-Mawdoo'ah*, vol. 1, p. 80.

[3] Ibid., pp. 78-79 and pp. 82-83.

[4] Ibid., p. 81.

[5] Soorah al-Anfaal (8):46.

[6] Soorah ar-Room (30):31-32.

Implicitly, too, Allaah has forbidden it, for example,

$$\text{﴿وَلَوْ شَاءَ رَبُّكَ لَجَعَلَ ٱلنَّاسَ أُمَّةً وَٰحِدَةً وَلَا يَزَالُونَ مُخْتَلِفِينَ ۝ إِلَّا مَن رَّحِمَ رَبُّكَ﴾}$$

"If your Lord had so willed, He could have made man-kind one people; but they will not cease to dispute, except those on whom your Lord has bestowed His mercy." [1]

If Allaah's mercy puts an end to dispute among men as is implied in the above, how then could disagreement and dispute be a mercy? In the unmistakable terms of the following verse and others like it, Allaah has ordered unity and agreement:

$$\text{﴿وَٱعْتَصِمُوا بِحَبْلِ ٱللَّهِ جَمِيعًا وَلَا تَفَرَّقُوا ۚ وَٱذْكُرُوا نِعْمَتَ ٱللَّهِ عَلَيْكُمْ إِذْ كُنتُمْ أَعْدَاءً فَأَلَّفَ بَيْنَ قُلُوبِكُمْ فَأَصْبَحْتُم بِنِعْمَتِهِ إِخْوَانًا﴾}$$

"Hold fast to the rope of Allaah together and do not split up. And remember Allaah's mercy on you when you were enemies, then He put love in your hearts and with His blessing you all became brothers." [2]

Differences Among the Ṣaḥaabah

In view of these clear Qur'anic condemnations, how then do we account for the disagreement which occured at times among the Prophet's (ﷺ) companions *(Sahaabah)* and the early scholars of *Fiqh*?

The differences of opinion which occurred among the Ṣaḥaabah were for the most part natural and unavoidable. A large portion of it was due to their different reasoning abilities which showed up in their various interpretations of Qur'anic verses and *Hadeeths*. There were

---

[1] Soorah Hood (11):118-119.

[2] Soorah Aal 'Imraan (3):103.

other causes which led to differences during their time which later disappeared; for example, the wide distribution of *Hadeeths* made it impossible for any individual *Sāhaabee* to be aware of them all, and thus wrong decisions were bound to be made where information was lacking. Obviously, they cannot be blamed for these and similar mistakes, which were not intentional. Furthermore, it is clear that they readily corrected their wrong decisions when authentic information or more relevant evidence indicated that this should be done. It is this willingness to cast aside wrong decisions in the search for truth which excludes these conflicting rulings from the category of accursed disagreements. In this connection, the messenger of Allaah (ﷺ) had said,

"If a judge strives his utmost and makes a correct ruling, he receives two rewards, but if he strives and errs he still receives one."[1] Based on this *Hadeeth*, the *Sahaabah* are considered absolved from blame for conflicting rulings. However, any discrepencies apparent in their different rulings are not to be glorified and perpetuated. In fact they themselves disliked disagreements, as is shown in the following narration quoted by ash-Shaafi'ee's student, al-Muzanee: 'Umar ibn al-Khattaab, the second Righteous Caliph, got angry because of a dispute between the *Sahaabee*, Ubayy ibn Ka'b, and another *Sahaabee*, Ibn Mas'ood, over the performance of *Salaah* in a single piece of cloth. Ubayy considered it quite alright while Ibn Mas'ood felt that was so only when cloth was scarce. 'Umar angrily left his residence and declared, "Have two of Allaah's messenger's companions disagreed and they are among those whom the masses watch closely and imitate? Ubayy is correct and Ibn Mas'ood should desist! If I hear of anyone disputing about this matter after this point, I will deal with him."[2]

Indeed, the early scholars well aware of the causes of differences among the *Sahaabah* and the tendency for people to want to perpetuate them. Accordingly, they made definitive statements on the

---

[1] Narrated by 'Abdullah ibn 'Amr ibn al'Aas and collected by al-Bukhaaree *(Sahih Al-Bukhari*, (Arabic-English), vol. 4, p. 442, no. 667) and Muslim *(Sahih Muslim* (English Trans.), vol. 3, p. 930, no. 4261).

[2] *Jaami' Bayaan al-'Ilm*, vol. 2, pp. 83-4.

matter in an effort to stave off dogmatism and sectarianism based on conflicting rulings of the *Sahaabah*. The following are a few examples of their statements on this vital subject. Ibn al-Qaasim, who was among the main students of Imaam Maalik, said, *"I heard Maalik and al-Layth both say the following concerning the differences among the Sahaabah: 'People say there is leeway for them in it, but it is not so; it was a case of wrong and right rulings' ".*[1]

Ash-hab, another of Imaam Maalik's students, said, *"Maalik was once asked whether one was safe to follow a ruling related to him by reliable narrators who had heard it from companions of the Prophet (ﷺ). He replied, 'No, by Allaah, not unless it is correct: the truth is only one. Can two opposing opinions be simultaneously correct? The opinion which is correct can be only one.' "*[2]

Imaam ash-Shaafi'ee's student, al-Muzanee, put it this way, *"The companions of Allaah's Messenger (ﷺ) disagreed from time to time and declared each other mistaken. Some of them examined the statements of others and researched them thoroughly. Therefore, if all of them felt that whatever they said was correct, they would never have investigated each other's statements or declared each other mistaken."* Al-Muzanee also said, *"The following question should be put to the one who allows disagreement, claiming that if two scholars strive to arrive at a decision concerning the same incident one ruling that it is "Halaal" and the other that it is "Haraam", both are correct. 'Are you basing that judgement on a fundamental text (the Qur'aan or the Sunnah) or on Qiyaas (analogical deduction)?' If he claims that it is based on a fundamental text, he should then be asked, 'How could it be based on a fundamental text when the Qur'aan, (which is the major fundamental text) condemns disagreement?' If he claims that it is by Qiyaas, he should be asked, 'How could the fundamental text reject dispute and you in turr*

---

[1] *Jaami' Bayaan al-'Ilm*, vol. 2, pp. 81-82.

[2] Ibid., vol. 2, pp. 82, 88, 89.

deduce from it that dispute is allowed?' No common person capable of reason would allow that, much less a scholar."[1]

Although the Sahaabah differed in the application of some principles, they used to go to extremes to preserve an appearance of unity and avoid things which would divide their ranks. But, among later scholars and followers who blindly and dogmatically clung to the inherited *Madh-habs,* we find the complete opposite. As was previously mentioned, their differences at one point led to the splitting of their ranks over *Salaah* (formal prayer), the greatest pillar of Islaam after the two testimonies of belief.

Conservative sectarians among later scholars at times carried their differences even beyond that extreme, making rulings which struck at the very heart of the brotherhood and unity of Islaam. For example, Imaam Abu Haneefah alone among the early Imaams felt that *Eemaan* (belief) neither decreased nor increased; one either believed or he disbelieved.[2] On the basis of Abu Haneefah's opinion, a ruling was made by later scholars of the *Madh-hab* stating that if one is asked the question, "Are you a believer?" It is *Haraam* to reply, "I am a believer, if Allaah so wills it," as it implied that one is in doubt about the existence of his belief.[3] According to the *Ijmaa'* of the scholars,

---

[1] *Jaami' Bayaan al-'Ilm,* vol. 2, p. 89.

[2] The position is at variance with both Qur'aan and *Hadeeth.* Allaah described true believers as **"Those whose Eemaan increases when people tell them to beware the (enemy) which has gathered to attack them"** (3:173). Elsewhere we find, **"And if His signs are read to them, their Eemaan increases."** (8:2) The Prophet (ﷺ) also said, *"None of you believes until I become more beloved to him than his offspring, father, and all mankind."* The negation here is taken to be a negation of perfection and not a negation of existence; otherwise, none of us could be considered Muslims. The *Hadeeth* is collected by al-Bukhaaree and Muslim. See *Sahih Al-Bukhari* (Arabic-English), vol. 1, p. 20, no. 14 and *Sahih Muslim* (English Trans.), vol. 1, p. 31, no. 71.

[3] This line of reasoning is clearly contradicted by the following *Hadeeth* in which the Prophet (ﷺ) taught us to make the following prayer at =

doubt about one's belief is equivalent to disbelief *(Kufr)*. Therefore, one should reply, "I am truly a believer".[1] The implied but unstated meaning of this ruling was that the followers of the other schools of thought were in doubt about their *Eemaan* and thus in disbelief. This was never stated by the early Hanafee school, but some later scholars deduced from it the ruling that followers of the Hanafee *Madh-hab* were prohibited from marrying followers of the Shaafi'ee *Madh-hab* which was the second most prominent *Madh-hab* at that time. This deduction was later over-ruled by scholars of the Hanafee *Madh-hab*,[2] but stands as historical evidence documenting the dangers of sectarianism.

= graveyards: *"Peace be on the believing and submitting people of these abodes, may Allaah have mercy on our predecessors and our successors. And, **Allaah willing,** we will be joining you all"* (Reported by 'Aa'eshah and collected by Muslim and Abu Daawood. See *Sahih Muslim* (English Trans.), vol. 2, pp. 461-2, no. 2127 and *Sunan Abu Dawud* (English Trans.), vol. 2, pp. 919-20, no. 3231). The Prophet ( ) was not in doubt about dying.

---

[1] Ibn Abee al-'Izz. *Sharh al-'Aqeedah at-Tahaaweeyah*, (Beirut: al-Maktab al-Islaamee, first edition, 1972), pp. 395-397.

[2] The new ruling was made by the famous Hanafee scholar titled, "Muftee ath-Thaqalayn", who allowed the marriage of Shaafi'ite women on the basis of the allowance of marriage to Christian and Jewish women (Zayn ad-Deen ibn Nujaym, quoted by the 16th century Egyptian Hanafee scholar in his eight volume work entitled *al-Bahr ar-Raa'iq)*. However, this ruling implied that Hanafite women were still not allowed to marry Shaafi'ite men just as they cannot marry Christian and Jewish men!

Section Summary

1. The position of the generality of Muslims is that the four *Madh-habs* are infallible, everyone must follow one of them and followers must not change *Madh-habs* or pick rulings from other *Madh-habs*.[1]

2. One who does not subscribe to the infallibility of the *Madh-habs* or does not follow any of the four *Madh-habs* is commonly, but mistakenly classified as a heretic and mislabelled either *"Wahhabi"* or *"Ahl-i Hadeeth"*.

3. The *Hadeeths* used to defend *Madh-hab* sectarianism are either misinterpreted or unauthentic.

4. The Qur'aan explicitly and implicitly condemns conflict and dispute among Muslims.

5. Differences among the *Sahaabah* were due to varying interpretational abilities and the extent to which they were exposed to *Hadeeths* of the Prophet (ﷺ). Their different rulings were not rigidly clung to in the face of evidence to the contrary.

6. Early scholars emphasized the fact that only those rulings of the *Sahaabah* which were proven to be correct in the long run were to be followed as correct.

7. Disagreements among the *Sahaabah* never led to disunity and division amongst them, whereas, among later scholars of the *Madh-hab*, differences evolved into disharmony among Muslims.

---

[1] *Under the heading* **Math-hab of the Convert** *the author of* Taqleed and Ijtihād *writes:* "If such a person lives in a place where a particular *Math-hab* is dominant, then he shall follow the *Math-hab* by virtue of its dominance. If he happens to be in a place where several *Mathā-hib* are in operation on a more or less equivalent basis, then he will be free to choose any *Math-hab* acceptable to him. *However, once the choice is made, he will be obliged to remain steadfast on the Math-hab of his choice.*" (p. 13)

11 CONCLUSION

From the preceding chapters we have seen that the *Madh-hab* has gone through four basic stages as a result of the effects of the following factors: conditions of the Muslim state (unity, disunity), status of religious leadership (unified and orthodox, or fragmented and unorthodox) and communication among scholars. When the state was a single body, the leadership was unified and orthodox, and Muslim scholars were close to each other thereby facilitating communication. At that time there was only one *Madh-hab*, whether that of the Prophet (ﷺ) or that of each of the Righteous Caliphs. There followed a breakdown of political and religious leadership within the relatively unified state (under Umayyad and 'Abbaasid rule), and the dispersion of the leading scholars throughout the empire. Consequently, a large number of *Madh-habs* arose as scholars in various parts of the state were obliged to make rulings without benefit of that close consultation which had existed when communication was not a problem. Characteristically, these scholars managed to retain the flexibility of former times, readily discarding their individual rulings in favor of the rulings of others which were based on more authentic or comprehensive *Hadeeths*. Subsequently, in the latter part of the 'Abbaasid dynasty, scholars were caught up in the political rivalry resulting from the splintering of state leadership. The situation was further aggravated by the official promotion of court debates which brought special royal favors to individual winners and their *Madh-habs*. Thereafter, it was but a step to fanatical sectarianism for which many of the followers of the four surviving *Madh-habs* became noted.

Dynamic *Fiqh*

The situation today is a mixture of the preceding stages. Mass communication has brought Muslim scholars into close contact once again, but religious leadership at the state level disappeared long ago when the Muslim world became divided into nationalist entities each with its own politico-economic governmental system. The vastly increased Muslim population of today (variously estimated between 800 million and a billion) has been held together by their belief in Allaah and His

Prophet (ﷺ) and by their commitment to the Qur'aan and the Sunnah. Religious leadership such as there is tends to be exercised in separate states through one of the four *Madh-habs,* which though less fanatic than formerly, unfortunately continue to be sectarian and hence divisive.

However, there have been encouraging signs, especially since the middle of this century, that the drive towards unity divinely built into Islaam is propelling Muslims the world over towards a revival of their religion as the decisive factor in their lives at the personal, communal and national levels. Given the multiplicity of cultures represented in the Muslim population and the increasing diversity of issues and problems arising from daily living in this rapidly changing world, many Muslims scholars have long felt that the goal of re-establishing Islaam as the supreme guide in the daily lives of Muslims, anywhere in the world, is achievable only by a revival of a dynamic *Fiqh* such as was practised in what we previously described as the **"Stage of Flowering".** This implies a reunification of the *Madh-habs* with all traces of fanaticism and sectarianism removed, and the revival of *Ijtihaad* to make *Fiqh* once more a dynamic, objectively deduced body of laws so that individual Muslim scholars and jurists may effectively and uniformly apply the *Sharee'ah* in all parts of the Muslim world, no matter what the socio-political-economic conditions.

No less important is the possible impact of such a reformation, not only on new converts to Islaam, but also on the new generation of Muslims born into the faith. In the case of the former, they would be spared the perplexing effects of conflicting rulings from *Madh-hab* to *Madh-hab,* while in the case of the latter, they would be spared the frustration of the sectarianism generated by *Madh-hab* contradictions and avoid the tendency towards total rejection of the *Madh-habs* and the outstanding contributions of early scholars.

Proposed Steps

Finally, a unified *Madh-hab* and a dynamic body of *Fiqh* envisioned above are felt to be needed in order to evolve vibrant Islamic communities and unite such communites throughout the world in the types of co-operative endeavors that would protect the common interest of mankind and project Islaam on a global scale. Assuming the desirability and validity of the twin goals of unifying the *Madh-habs* and re-establishing a dynamic *Fiqh*, what are the steps that might be taken towards achieving these goals? In the first place, concerted efforts will have to be made to resolve in a truly objective way the differences between the existing *Madh-habs* and their predecessors, using the methodology of the early scholars as defined by their statements and practices quoted in the previous chapters.

The mechanics of initiating appropriate action calls for enlightened leadership springing from the ranks of progressive and influential scholars of high calibre, that is, some person or persons imbued with the zeal to effect changes along the lines proposed will have to take the initiative to communicate with other interested parties with a view to planning and organizing the procedural details. Drawing on modern day systems approaches to problem solving, these steps would include: objective definition of the real obstacles to solution; selection of the most appropriate solution; determination of possible methods of implementation; selection of the most appropriate method; then putting the solution into effect. At each stage in this type of planning, the steps chosen would have to be continuously evaluated with regard to the problems and the goals. Obviously, the task of unifying the *Madh-habs,* and restoring dynamic *Fiqh* are not susceptible to simplistic solutions, but with Allaah's blessing they are within the realm of possibility.

On a theoretical level, it is comparatively easy to make suggestions for the resolution of interpretational and applicational differences among *Madh-habs.* The following framework, based on the methodology of the early Imaams, has been recommended at various times by progressive-minded Islamic scholars.

Contradictory and Variational Differences

Differences among *Madh-hab's* rulings fall into two main categories; **firstly,** contradictory differences *(Ikhtilaaf Taḍaadd),* totally opposite rulings which can not logically be simultaneously correct, for example rulings in which one *Madh-hab* defines something as *Halaal* and another defines it as *Haraam*,[1] and **secondly,** variational differences *(Ikhtilaaf Tanawwu'),* conflicting rulings which are logically acceptable variations which can co-exist, for example, various sitting positions used by the Prophet (ﷺ) in *Salaah* some of which have been preferred over others by the different *Madh-habs.* In many cases of differences arising from meanings (literal and figurative) of words and grammatical constructions, there are authentic *Hadeeths* which specify the meanings intended and these specified meanings should be given preference over all other interpretations. Similarly, legal rulings which were made in the absence of *Hadeeths,* or based on weak narrations or made according to conditions which eliminated authentic narrations, should be regarded as invalid and should be replaced by the rulings of other jurists which were made on the basis of authentic *Hadeeths.* As for rulings based on controversial principles or unrestricted *Qiyaas,* these should be objectively examined in the light of the fundamental principles of the Qur'aan, the Sunnah and the *Ijmaa'* of the *Sahaabah;* rulings agreeing with these fundamentals should then be accepted and those contradicting them should then be rejected. Outside the scope of the foregoing suggested solutions, there remain a number of issues on which there is more than one ruling equally supported by the Qur'aan, the *Hadeeth,* the *Ijmaa'* of the *Sahaabah* or *Qiyaas.* The different rulings in such cases should be treated as viable options to be applied according to circumstances and these are a part of the logically acceptable variations mentioned as the second category of differences in *Madh-hab* rulings.

This framework for the resolution of differences among the *Madh-habs* could best be effected within institutions devoted to the objective study of *Fiqh;* that is, institutions of learning in which no *Madh-hab* is given preference over another. Islamic law could then be studied from its primary sources, and the positions of the various *Madh-habs* could then be analysed rationally and objectively as outlined previously. If the standard of scholarship in such centers of learning were high, the enormous task of re-unifying the *Madh-habs* could then be undertaken with excellent prospects for eventual success. A single *Madh-hab* completely free from sectarianism and firmly based on sound scholarship, could provide not only trustworthy and continuing leadership for the Muslim world in general, but also concrete guidance to various reformist movements aimed at re-establishing divine law as the only valid basis for governing Muslim countries. With success in the area of the *Madh-hab* reunification and the establishment of divine law, we could then look towards the reunification of the *Ummah*, the Muslim nation, and the re-establishment of the *Khilaafah*, the true caliphate. This would provide the necessary foundation for the execution of Allaah's law throughout the earth, if Allaah so wills it.

GLOSSARY

In this glossary the correct forms of the Arabic plurals are shown in brackets after the singular form or vice versa where the plural is the commonly used form, however in the text Arabic terms are pluralized using the English s-form.

Aadaab (sing. Adab): Islamic etiquette.

'Abbaasid: The second major dynasty of Muslim caliphs which began with the accession of Caliph Abul-'Abbaas as-Saffaah (750-754 CE) and ended with the murder of Caliph al-Musta'sim (1242-1258 CE) at the hands of the Mongols.

Ahl al-Hadeeth (lit. Hadeeth people): The name given to early scholars who preferred to avoid excessive reasoning and instead relied heavily upon the *literal* interpretations of sayings and actions of the Prophet (ﷺ). In more recent times in India and Pakistan it became a derogatory term used for those who opposed the blind following of any *Madh-hab*.

Ahl ar-Ra'i (lit. Opinion people): The name given to early scholars who used extensive reasoning in the interpretation of the sayings and actions of the Prophet (ﷺ).

Athar (pl. Aathaar): A saying or ruling of the *Sahaabah* and their students.

'Aql (pl. 'Uqool, lit. mind or intelligence): The process by which Islamic laws are determined based upon what the intellect considers good, and what it considers bad.

Bay': Business transactions.

Bid'ah: Innovation in religious rites and principles.

C.E. (i.e. Christian Era) is used instead of A.D. (Anno Domini, lit. in the year of our Lord) because Islaam does not recognize Jesus, the son of Mary, as the Lord but as a prophet of God.

Da'eef (lit. weak): When applied to *Hadeeth*, it means that it is unreliable due to a deficiency in one or more of its narrators, or a break in the chain of narrators.

DHaahir (pl. DHawaahir): The obvious literal meaning of a Qur'anic or *Hadeethic* text.

Du'aa (pl. Ad'eyah): Informal prayer which has no particular format or time limitations.

Eemaan (lit. faith): Correct belief in Islaam.

Faasiq: A Muslim who intentionally and repeatedly breaks Islamic law.

Fatwaa (pl. Fataawaa): A legal ruling on an issue of religious importance.

Fiqh: The understanding and application of *Sharee'ah* (divine law).

Furoo' (sing. Far'): Secondary principles of Islamic law deduced from the primary principles.

Hadeeth (pl. Ahaadeeth): A saying, action or approval of the Prophet (ﷺ).

Hajj: A compulsory duty on all adult Muslims of sound mind and body once in a lifetime if they are economically able. Hajj may be defined as Pilgrimage to the Ka'bah in Makkah during the months of *Shawaal*, *Dhul-Qa'dah* and *Dhul-Hijjah* (10th, 11th and 12th months of the lunar calendar) in order to perform certain prescribed rites of worship there.

Halaal: The name of the legal category of things which are permissible. It includes things which are classified *Waajib* (compulsory), *Mustahabb* (recommended), *Mubaah* (allowed) and *Makrooh* (disliked).

Haraam: The name given to the legal category of things which are forbidden in Islaam.

Hijaaz: The western coastline of the Arabian peninsula, which includes the cities of Makkah and Madeenah .

Ijmaa': The unanimous agreement of the *Sahabah* [companions of the Prophet (ﷺ)], or scholars in general, on a point of Islamic law.

Ijtihaad (pl. Ijtihaadaat): The reasoning process by which Islamic laws are deduced after thorough research.

Imaam (pl. A'immah): Literally a leader, but Islamically it refers to one who leads a congregation in prayer or an outstanding scholar.

Istihsaan (lit. preference): The preference of one proof over another proof because the former appears more suitable to the situation than the latter, even though the preferred proof may be technically weaker than the one it is preferred to. This may involve the preference of a *Hadeeth* which is specific over a general one, or it may even involve the preference of a more suitable law over the one deduced by *Qiyaas*. An application of the principle of *Istihsaan* is seen in the treatment of a contract for manufacture and sale of an item. According to *Qiyaas* and based on the Prophet's statement, *"Whoever sells food should not do so until he has it in his possession"*[1] contracts for manufacture are invalid since the item is non-existent at the time of the contract. However, since such contracts have been universally accepted by people and the need for such contracts is obvious, the ruling by *Qiyaas* was dropped and the contracts were allowed based on the principle of preference, that is, *Istihsaan*.

Istis-haab (lit. seeking a link): Refers to a process of deducing *Fiqh* laws by linking a later set of circumstances with an earlier. It is based on the assumption that the *Fiqh* laws applicable to certain conditions remain valid so long as it is not certain that these conditions have altered. If, for example, on account of the long absence of someone, it is doubtful whether he is alive or dead, then by *Istis-haab* all rules must remain in force which would hold if one knew for certain that he was still alive.

Istislaah (lit. seeking the welfare): The principle of *Istihsaan* developed by Abu Haneefah was also applied by Maalik and his students in a more restricted form and called by the name *Istislaah*, which simply means seeking that which is more suitable to human welfare. It deals with things which have not been specifically considered by the *Sharee'ah*, but which are aimed at in the Divine Law. An example of *Istislaah* is found in Caliph 'Alee's ruling that every member of a group who took part in a murder was guilty even though only one of the group had actually committed the act of murder. The legal texts of *Sharee'ah* covered only the actual murderer. Another example is the right of a Muslim leader to collect taxes from the rich other than *Zakaah*, if the interest of the state demands it; whereas, in *Sharee'ah*

Reported by Ibn 'Umar and collected by Maalik (*Muwaṭṭa Imam Malik*, (English Trans.), p. 296, no. 1324).

only *Zakaah* has been specified. Imaam Maalik also applied the principle of *Istislaah* to deduce laws more in keeping with human needs than those deduced by *Qiyaas*.

Ittibaa': Following the *Madh-habs* based on knowledge or inquiry, without fanaticism.

Jama': In the field of *Hadeeth* it is combining the meanings of two apparently contradicting *Hadeeths* in such a way that one explains a detail of the other.

Janaabah: Ritual impurity caused by sexual intercourse or wet-dream.

Jihaad: War fought to spread Islaam whether it be physical, psychological or spiritual. However, the term is most commonly used in reference to actual battle.

Kadhdhaab (lit. a compulsive liar): In the field of *Hadeeth* science, it is the name given to a narrator of *Hadeeths* who was known to lie.

Khamr (lit. fermented grape juice): In Islamic law it refers to all intoxicants.

Khaleefah (pl. Khulafaa): The title given to the leader of all Muslims.

Khawaarij (sing. Khaarijee, lit. the seceders): A part of the army of Caliph 'Alee ibn Abee Taalib broke off during the battle of Siffeen (657 CE). This battle was between 'Alee and Mu'aawiyah ibn Abee Sufyaan who had refused to accept 'Alee as Caliph. When arbitrations were held between the two sides in order to stop the bloodshed, a large group from among 'Alee's followers, who were mainly from the tribe of Tameem, broke off in opposition and elected 'Abdullaah ibn Wahb ar-Raasibee as their leader. They declared both 'Alee and Mu'aawiyah *Kaafirs* (disbelievers) because, in their opinion, the two of them had sought human arbitration over what was ordained by Divine law. They also branded everyone *Kaafir* (infidel) who did not accept their point of view and disown 'Alee as well as Mu'aawiyah. The *Khawaarij* felt that all arbitration should come directly from Qur'aan. As a result of their position, they permitted the spilling of any Muslim's blood who opposed them and they allowed the confiscation of their wealth. They also forbade their members from marrying or inheriting from non-*Khaarijee* Muslims. According to the beliefs of the *Khawaarij* anyone who has committed a major sin (fornication, lying, intoxication, etc.) is regarded as an apostate. Their extreme wing, the *Azraqees,* said that anyone who has become a *Kaafir* in this way can never re-enter the faith and should be killed for his apostasy along with his wives and children. Caliph 'Alee was forced to attack them in their camp and inflicted a terrible defeat on them in which Ibn Wahb and the majority of his followers were slain (battle of Nahrawaan 657 CE). However, the victory cost 'Alee dearly. Not only was the rebellion far from being suppressed, it was prolonged in a series of local uprisings in the following two years. 'Alee himself perished by the dagger of a *Khaarijee,* 'Abdur-Rahmaan ibn Muljam, the husband of a woman whose family had lost most of its members at Nahrawaan.

Madh-hab (pl. Madhaahib): A school of thought whether legal or philosophical.

Mash-hoor (lit. famous): In reference to *Hadeeths,* it means a saying or action of the Prophet (器) which is well known, having been narrated by many people from a variety of sources.

Masjid (pl. Masaajid): House of worship in Islaam, also called Mosque.

Mu'akhkhar: The later portion of the dowry which is paid in the case of death or divorce.

Muftee: A scholar able to give legal rulings on old or new situations.

MunaadHaraat (sing. MunaadHarah): The name given to debates between scholars of various *Madh-habs* on Islamic legal issues.

Munaafiq (pl. Munaafiqoon): One who pretends to be a Muslim, but in fact disbelieves in Islaam.

Muqaddam: The portion of the dowry *(mahr)* which is given before marriage according to the tradition in some countries.

Mursal: A *Hadeeth* attributed to the Prophet (器) by a student of the *Sahaabah* in which the name of the narrator *(Sahaabee)* is deleted.

Mustahabb: A highly recommended act for which there is a reward if it is done, but no punishment if left undone. Also known as Sunnah.

Mu'tazilite (Anglicized version of *Mu'tazilee):* A follower of the philosophical school of thought commonly called rationalism. This school was founded by Waasil ibn 'Ataa and 'Amr ibn 'Ubayd during the eighth century CE. It later became the official philosophy of the 'Abbaasid state and an inquisition was instituted in order to force all scholars to abide by it. However, Caliph Mutawakkil (1177-1192 CE) abandoned it and lifted the inquisition. Among its more notable principles were the belief that Allaah was everywhere, the belief that the Qur'aan was created and only its meanings were divine, that Allaah would not be seen by the people of Paradise, that man has free will without divine interference, and that one who commits a major sin enters a state between belief and disbelief.

Nahw: Grammar.

Qaadee (pl. Qudaah): A judge.

Qiyaas: Analogical deduction of Islamic laws. New laws are deduced from earlier laws based on a similarity between their causes.

Qur' (pl. Quroo'): The menses or the period of purity between menses.

Sahaabah (sing. Sahaabee): Anyone who saw the Prophet Muhammad (鑅) and died a Muslim. Commonly translated as companions.

Saheeh (lit. accurate): In the science of *Hadeeth* it refers to a *Hadeeth* which has a continuous chain of narrators (each narrator having met the one he narrated from) in which each narrator is known to have been righteous and known to have had a good memory.

Salaah (pl. Salawaat): Formal prayer consisting of standing, bowing, sitting and prostrating during which certain specific prayers are recited.

Sawm: Fasting from dawn to sunset by abstaining from food, drink, sex and all immoral acts (e.g. lying, swearing etc). Also written *Siyaam*.

Shee'ah (commonly spelled Shia' or Shi'ites): At the beginning of Yazeed ibn Mu'aawiyah's reign, Husayn, son of the fourth Caliph 'Alee ibn Abee Taalib, rose in revolt against his leadership. 'Alee ibn Abee Taalib's followers in Iraq had invited Husayn to Iraq to lead the revolt, but they later deserted him and caused his death at the hands of Yazeed's soldiers at Karbalaa (680 CE). In their anguish, many of those who considered themselves to be followers of 'Alee, deviated from the mainstream of Islaam. They became excessive in expressing their love for 'Alee and their hatred for all who opposed him. They declared the first three Caliphs, Abu Bakr, 'Umar and 'Uthmaan, to be *Kaafirs* (disbelievers) who had stolen the office of Imaam from 'Alee. All of *Sahaabah* [companions of the Prophet (ﷺ)] were declared apostates due to their ratification of the first three Caliphs' caliphate and only Salmaan al-Faarisee, Abu Dharr al-Ghifaaree and Miqdaad ibn al-Aswad al-Kindee (some accounts give a few more names) were spared this grave accusation, because they were supposed to have championed 'Alee's right to caliphate on the death of the Prophet (ﷺ). To support this claim, *Hadeeths* were invented in which the Prophet (ﷺ) made all of his followers and companions swear an oath of allegiance to 'Alee that he would be their leader after the Prophet's (ﷺ) death. This incident was supposed by them, to have taken place at *Ghadeer Khum* on the way back to Madeenah from Makkah after the farewell Hajj on the 18th of Dhul-Hijjah, 10 A.H. They also claimed that only certain blood descendants of the Prophet Muhammad (ﷺ) by way of his cousin 'Alee and the Prophet's daughter, Faatimah, had the right to be the leader *(Imaam)* of all Muslims. They even went so far as to attribute to these descendants, whom they entitled *Imaams,* some of God's unique qualities and elevate them above the Prophets of God. Aayatullah Roohullah Khomeini expressed these beliefs as follows: "The Imaam has an exalted position, an elevated rank and a creational vicegerency (caliphate) to whose sovereignty and dominion all of the atoms of the universe yield and obey. And, among the basic tenets of our *Madhhab (Shee'ah)* is that the Imaams have a station which can not be attained by either an angel close (to God)[1] or a commissioned Prophet. And furthermore, based on the narrations and *Hadeeths* which we have, the greatest Prophet (Muhammad) (ﷺ) and the (Twelve) Imaams existed before this world (was created) as lights which Allaah made encircle His throne."[2]

---

[1] Mistranslated as "Cherubim" in *Islam and Revolution* U.S.A: (Mizan Press, 1981) by Hamid Algar.

[2] Khomeini, *al-Hukoomah al-Islaameeyah* (1398 AH/1969 CE) Arabic edition, published in Tehran 1980, p. 52.

However, in the designation of each new Imaam, new Shi'ite sects emerged among the followers who were displeased and rejected the choice. Hence, historically, there were many Shi'ite sects holding innumerable beliefs. And it should be noted that most of the heretical sects which split off from Islaam had their origins in one or another of the Shi'ite sects. For example, the *Nusayree* sect founded by Muhammad ibn Nusayr who claimed in the year 855 CE that 'Alee was a manifestation of God,[1] the *Druze* sect founded by Muhammad ibn Ismaa'eel ad-Durzee who claimed that the Faatimid Shi'ite Caliph of Egypt, al-Haakim bi Amrillaah (966-1021 CE) was the last manifestation of God in human form, and the *Bahai* sect formed by 'Alee Muhammad Ridaa (the *Baab*) who claimed prophethood and his disciple Husayn 'Alee (*Bahaa-ullaah*) who claimed that he was the awaited Christ and that Allaah was manifest in him.

Shirk: Associating partners with God by giving God's attributes to created things or giving God the attributes of created things.

Shooraa: Mutual consultation or consultative government.

Sujood: Prostration in *Salaah.*

Sunnah: The way of life of the Prophet (ﷺ), consisting of his sayings, actions and silent approvals. The Sunnah of the Prophet (ﷺ) is contained in the various narrations of *Hadeeth. Sunnah* is also used to mean a recommended deed as opposed to *Fard*, or *Waajib* a compulsory one.

Sunnee: (Commonly written sunni or sunnite): One who follows the Sunnah of the Prophet (ﷺ), that is, a follower of orthodox or mainstream Islaam. This term is usually used to distinguish between the various deviant sects and the pure message of Islaam.

Taabi'oon (sing. Taabi'ee, lit. follower): Those who met and studied under the *Sahaabah* and died as Muslims.

Tafseer: An explanation of the meanings of the Qur'anic verses.

Tahaarah: Islamic hygiene involving purification of the body, clothes and place of worship according to set rites.

---

[1] This sect is also known as Alawis. The ruling tribe of Syria and the country's president, Hafiz Asad, belong to it.

Talaaq: Divorce. In Islaam there are two types of divorce - *Talaaq Raj'ee* in which the woman may be taken back without the necessity of a new marriage and *Talaaq Baa'in* in which the woman can not be returned until she marries and divorces another man.

Taqleed: The blind following of a particular *Madh-hab* (school of Islamic legal thought).

Taqwaa: The protection of self from the wrath of God by doing what He has commanded and avoiding what He has forbidden. It is also taken to mean God-consciousness.

Tarjeeh: Giving preference to one narration of *Hadeeth* or a statement of a scholar over another narration on the same topic due to the greater authenticity of the former.

Tas-heeh: Authentification and classification of statements made by scholars of a *Madh-hab* or the verification of the authenticity of a *Hadeeth*.

Tawassul: Seeking the intervention of intermediaries in one's prayers to God.

Tawheed: The purely unitarian concept of God, found only in Islaam, in which Allaah (God) is considered as being uniquely one in His essence, qualities and actions.

Tayammum: Ritual purification with dust in the absence of water.

'Ulamaa (sing. 'Aalim): Literally scholars, but commonly used to refer to Islamic scholars.

Umayyad: The first major dynasty of Muslim caliphs which began in the year 661 CE with the ascension of Caliph Mu'aawiyah and ended with the demise of Caliph Marwaan II (744-750 CE)

Ummah (pl. Ummam): Literally nation but commonly used to mean the Muslim nation which has neither geographic boundaries nor a national language.

'Urf: Custom or tradition common to an area or people incorporated into Islamic law. Local custom may become a secondary source of law if it does not contradict any of the basic principles of Islamic law, for example, local marriage customs. Islamically the dowry *(Mahr)* must be agreed upon as part of the marriage contract, but it has no set time in which it has to be paid. However, it is the custom of Egyptians as well as others that a portion of it, called the *Muqaddam*, must be paid before the marriage ceremony while the remainder, called *Mu'akhkhar*, is only required to be paid in the case of death or divorce according to whichever occurs first.

Another example of '*Urf* may be found in rental customs. Islamic law does not require the payment of a price until the thing being sold has been delivered completely. However, it is the accepted practice that rent is paid before the rented place or object has been used for the agreed time period. Yet another example concerns a custom in Syria where, the word *Daabbah* means a horse; whereas, its general meaning in Arabic is a four-legged animal. Hence, a contract made in Syria requiring payment in the form of a *Daabbah* would legally mean a horse whereas elsewhere in the Arab world it would have to be more clearly defined as a horse.

Uṣool (sing. Aṣl): The fundamental principles of any science or field of study. For example, *Uṣool al-Fiqh* are the basic sources of Islamic law, the Qur'aan, the Sunnah, *Ijmaa'* and *Qiyaas*.

Wuḍoo: A ritual state of purity stipulated as a precondition for certain acts of worship. Usually translated as ablution. It involves washing of the arms to the elbows, washing the face and wiping the hair, and washing the feet up to the ankles.

Zakaah: A compulsory form of charity collected once per year by the Islamic state from each Muslim member who has surplus wealth over and above his/her basic needs which has remained in his/her possession for at least a year, if that surplus wealth is more than a designated minimum (approx. $ 1000 U.S.).

Az-Zubayr, 'Abdullaah ibn: Toward the end of Caliph Yazeed ibn Mu'aawiyah's reign (680-683 CE), 'Abdullaah ibn az-Zubayr was declared Caliph in Hijaaz. Upon learning of this rebellion, Yazeed sent an army commanded by his general, Muslim ibn 'Uqbah, to quell the revolt. The army sacked Madeenah in 683 CE on its way to Makkah. However, before it reached Makkah, its commander died and al-Ḥuṣayn ibn Numayr took charge. The army then laid siege to the Holy city of Makkah and catapults were set up on the hills surrounding the city. Huge boulders were rained on the masjid eventually causing the collapse of some of the walls of the Ka'bah and the splitting of the Black Stone itself. However, during the siege, Caliph Yazeed died and the Umayyad army was withdrawn. Iraq then joined the revolt of Ibn az-Zubayr against Umayyad rule and Ibn az-Zubayr's brother, Mus'ab, was made its Ameer (governor). Shortly after that, Southern Arabia, Egypt and parts of Syria also joined Caliph Ibn az-Zubayr and he was requested to leave Makkah in order to consolidate his command. However, Ibn az-Zubayr was reluctant to leave the Holy City. When Marwaan ibn al-Hakam (683-685 CE) assumed leadership of the Umayyad dynasty, Damascus and Syria were once again brought under Umayyad rule. Hijaaz remained under the rule of Caliph Ibn az-Zubayr until Marwaan's son and successor, 'Abdul-Malik (685-705 CE), sent his iron-handed general, al-Hajjaaj ibn Yoosuf at the head of an enormous Syrian army which gave the coup de grace to the counter-caliphate. Beginning March 25, 692 CE, al-Hajjaaj pressed the siege against Makkah for six and a half months. Inspired by the heroic exhortation of his mother, Asmaa, (daughter of Abu Bakr and sister of 'Aa'eshah), Ibn az-Zubayr fought valiantly on until he was slain. His head was removed and sent to Damascus and his body, after hanging for some time on public display, was delivered to his aged mother. With the death of Ibn az-Zubayr one of the last champions of the old faith passed away and the Muslim world in its entirety fell under the iron fist of the Umayyads.

INDEX OF ḤADEETHS

BIBLIOGRAPHY

Abu Zahrah, Muhammad, *Taareekh al-Madhaahib al-Islaameeyah*, (Cairo: Daar al-Fikr al'Arabee).

al-A'dHamee, Mustafa, *Saheeh Ibn Khuzaymah*, (Beirut: al-Maktab al-Islaamee, 1st ed., 1978).

al-Albaanee, Muhammad Naasir ad-Deen, *Da'eef al-Jaami' as-Sagheer* (Beirut: al-Maktab al-Islaamee, 1979).

------------, *Irwaa al-Ghaleel* (Beirut: al-Maktab al-Islaamee, 1st ed., 1979).

------------, *Saheeh Sunan Abee Daawood*, (Beirut: al-Maktab al-Islaamee, 1st ed., 1988).

------------, *Sifah Salaah an-Nabee*, (Beirut: al-Maktab al-Islaamee, ninth ed. 1972).

------------, *Sisilah al-Ahaadeeth ad-Da'eefah wal-Maudoo'ah*, (Beirut: al-Maktab al-Islaamee 3rd. ed. 1972).

Bek, Muhammad al-Khidaree, *Taareekh at-Tashree' al-Islaamee*, (Cairo: al-Maktabah at-Tijaareeyah al-Kubraa, 1960).

ad-Dahlawee, Waleeyullaah, *al-Insaaf fee Bayaan Asbaab al-Ikhtilaaf*, (Beirut: Daar an-Nafaa'is 2nd. ed., 1978).

adh-Dhahabee, Muhammad Husein, *ash-Sharee'ah al-Islaameeyah*, (Egypt: Daar al-Kutub al-Hadeethah, second edition, 1968).

al-Fulaanee, Saalih ibn Muhammad, *Eeqaadh Himam Ulil-Absaar lil-Iqtidaa bi Sayyid al-Muhaajireen wal-Ansaar*, (Cairo: al-Muneereeyah Press, 1935).

Hassan, Hassan Ibrahim, *Islam: a Religious Political, Social and Economic Study*, (Iraq: University of Baghdad Press, 1967).

Ibn 'Aabideen, Muhammad Faheem, *Haashiyah ibn 'Aabideen*, (Cairo: al-Maymaneeyah Press, 1833-1900).

Ibn Abee Haatim, 'Abdur-Rahmaan ibn Muhammad, *al-Jarh wat-Ta'deel*, (Hyderabad, India: Majlis Daairah al-Ma'aarif al-'Uthmaaneeyah: 1952).

Ibn Abee 'Izz, *Sharh al-'Aqeedah at-Tahaaweeyah*, (Beirut: al-Maktab al-Islaamee, 1st ed., 1972).

Ibn 'Abdul Barr, Yoosuf ibn 'Umar, *Jaami' Bayaan al-'Ilm*, (Cairo: al-Muneereeyah Press, 1927)

------------, *al-Intiqaa fee Fadaa'il ath-Thalaathah al-A'immah al-Fuqahaa*, (Cairo: Maktab al-Qudsee, 1931).

Ibn 'Asaakir, 'Alee ibn al-Haran, *Taareekh Dimishq al-Kabeer*, (Damascus: Rawdah ash-Shaam, 1911-1932).

Ibn Iraaq, 'Alee, *Tanzeeh ash-Sharee'ah al-Marfoo'ah* (Beirut: Daar al-Kutub al-'Ilmeeyah, 1979).

Ibn al-Jawzee, 'Abdur-Raheem ibn 'Alee, *Munaaqib al-Imaam Ahmad ibn Hambal*, (Beirut: Daar al-Aafaaq al-Jadeedah, second printing, 1977).

Ibn Mu'een, Yahyaa, *at-Taareekh*, (Makkah: King 'Abdul Aziz University, 1979).

Ibn al-Qayyim, Muhammad ibn Abee Bakr, *I'laam al-Mooqi'een*, (Egypt: Al-Haajj 'Abdus-Salaam Press, 1988).

Ibn Rushd, Muhammad ibn Ahmad, *Bidaayah al-Mujtahid wa Nihaayah al-Muqtasid*, (Egypt: al-Maktabah at-Tijaareeyah al-Kubraa).

Ibn Taymeeyah, Ahmad ibn 'Abdul-Haleem, *Raf'ul-Malaam 'an al-A'immah al-A'laam*, (Beirut: al-Maktab al-Islaamee, third e.d., 1970).

al-Jaboree, 'Abdullaah Muhammad, *Fiqh al-Imaam al-Awzaa'ee* (Baghdad, Iraq: Matba'ah al-Irshaad, 1977).

al-Khateeb al-Baghdaadee, Ahmad ibn 'Alee, *al-Kifaayah fee 'Ilm ar-Riwaayah*, (Cairo: Daar al-Kutub al-Hadeethah, 2nd ed., 1972).

Khomeini, Aayatullaah, *al-Hukoomah al-Islaameeyah*, (Tehran, 1969), Arabic edition.

Kramers, J.H. and Bill, H.A.R., *Shorter Encyclopedia of Islam*, (Ithaca, New York: Cornell University Press, 1953).

Moosaa, Muhammad Yoosuf, *Muhaadaraat fee Taareekh al-Fiqh al-Islaamee,* (Cairo: Daar al-Kitaab al-'Arabee, 1955).

an-Nawawee, Yahyaa ibn Sharaf ad-Deen, *Al-Majmoo' Sharh al-Muhadhdhab,* (Cairo: Idaarah at-Tabaa'ah al-Muneerah, 1925).

Qadri, Anwar Ahmad, *Islamic Jurisprudence in the Modern World,* (Lahore, Pakistan: Ashraf, Ist ed., 1963).

al-Qattaan, Mannaa', *Mabaahith fee 'Uloom al-Qur'aan,* (Riyadh: Maktab al-Ma'aarif, 8th ed., 1981).

------------, *at-Tashree' wa al-Fiqh fee al-Islaam,* (Egypt: Maktab Wahbah, Matba'ah Taqaddam, 1st. ed., 1976).

Rahimuddin, Mohammad, *Translation of Muwatta Imam Malik,* (New Delhi: Kitab Bhavan, 1st ed., 1981).

Saabiq, as-Sayyid, *Fiqh as-Sunnah,* (Beirut: Daar al-Kitaab al-'Arabee, 3rd. ed., 1977).

ash-Shak'ah, Mustafaa, *al-A'immah al-Arba'ah,* (Cairo: Daar al-Kitaab al-Misree, 1st. ed., 1979).

Shalabee, Muhammad Mustafaa, *Usool al-Fiqh al-Islaamee,* (Beirut, Lebanon: Daar an-Nahdah al-'Arabeeyah, 2nd. ed., 1978).

------------, *al-Madkhal fee at-Ta'reef bil-Fiqh al-Islaamee,* (Beirut: Daar an-Nahdah al-'Arabeeyah, 1969).

ash-Shawkaanee, Muhammad ibn 'Alee, *Nail al-Awtaar,* (Egypt: al-Halabee Press, 1st. ed.).

------------, *al-Fawaa'id al-Majmoo'ah* (Beirut: al-Maktab al-Islaamee, 2nd., 1972).

Sherwani, Maulana Muhammad Maseehullah Khan, *Taqleed and Ijtihaad,* (Port Elizabeth, South Africa: The Majlis, 1980).

Strzyzewska, Bozena Gajane, *Tareekh at-Tashree' al-Islaamee,* (Beirut, Lebanon: Daar al-Aafaaq al-Jadeedah, 1st ed., 1980).

at-Turkee, 'Abdullaah 'Abdul-Mushin, *Asbaab Ikhtilaaf al-Fuqahaa,* (Riyadh: as-Sa'aadah, 1st ed., 1974).